GEMS FROM THE GREEK
VOLUME II

BASIC
BIBLE
TRUTHS
PUBLICATIONS

2212 Bellevue Rd
Dublin, GA. 31021
basicbibletruth.org

Copyright © 2019
Johnie Scaggs, Jr.

Basic Bible Truths Publications

You may use this book as freely as you will, however, do not change anything the writer has written.

Introduction

It was my blessing and privilege to study first year New Testament Greek under Wayne Price.

After studying from Wayne, I took fifty-nine college hours of New Testament Greek. I have also written a book dealing with the Greek of 1,2,3 John. Even though I have two doctor's degrees in religion and five Master's degrees (four are in religion and one is in math education), I still yield to Wayne when it comes to Greek scholarship. Wayne received both the bachelor's and master's degrees in New Testament Greek around 1960 from Abilene Christian College. He has taught Greek for many years in Schools of Preaching in Oklahoma. His scholarship is outstanding!

In my opinion, more than his scholarship is his friendship! He is about twelve years older than me. I have called him many times asking for his help understanding the Scriptures. He has always been very kind and helpful to me. He has always demonstrated a loving, Christian attitude towards me. He never said I am too busy or call me later. He has been a great friend and mentor. He has always impressed me with his wisdom and knowledge of the Scriptures. I have been blessed by knowing Wayne. I am confident that many preachers and teachers of the Word say the same thing!

It is with my whole heart that I recommend this work by Wayne Price. I am sure many students will be blessed through the years by his writings after he has gone to glory. "He being dead yet speaketh."

Dr. John Hobbs

Forward

With this section which you are now reading, we begin volume 2 of <u>Gems from the Greek</u>. The Bible was written primarily in two languages, the Old Testament in Hebrew, and the New Testament in Greek, with a few sections and individual words in each containing some Aramaic expressions. In this 2nd volume, we continue to focus upon the New Testament, and the Greek language in which it was written.

Words are important since they convey thoughts from one person to another. This fact is of much greater significance when applied to the New Testament, since Deity (God, Christ, and the Holy Spirit) is involved using words to convey heaven's message to mankind (1 Corinthians 2:13). We plan to emphasize the importance of Holy Spirit selected words and how the choice of one word over another in the Greek New Testament plays an important role in Biblical interpretation.

When translating from one language to another, it is recognized by most linguists that there are finer shades of thought that often go untranslated. It is also true that oftentimes translators use synonyms to translate the same original Greek word, and as result, the pun (play on words) used by the inspired writers is totally missed. Guy N. Woods writes: "To mine these rich ores of truth, and make them shine and sparkle for one's hearers is surely the most fascinating and delightful of all studies. A preacher or Bible school teacher who is able to do this will always exhibit a freshness and charm that will delight and thrill his hearers…" (How to Read the Greek New Testament, pp. 11-12). Again, "the clearest, simplest, most vivid and most inspiring commentary on the New Testament in English is, to one who can use it, the New Testament in Greek" (*Ibid.*, p.13).

So many words in the original language are compound words, that is, they are made up of two or more other words, and the renderings of these terms often fails to bring out the richness of meaning involved. Furthermore, our English translations often fail to get across the idea of plurality or singularity when such Greek terms are translated into English. Why? Because the target language (English) often uses a word which is both plural and singular. For example, the pronoun "you" in English can be either plural or singular, but in the original it has to be either one or the other. Another example is the uses of the word "the dead" translating the Greek word nekron. Much of the time, this word is ablative plural in Greek, but is often rendered simply as "the dead" in English. This leaves the English reader, who knows no Greek, unaware that the Greek literally says, "from the dead **ones**."

Another well-known example is that used by the Apostle Paul in Galatians 1:6,7. The King James has Paul saying that he was amazed that the Galatian Christians had accepted "*another gospel, which is not another…*" Instead of being abstract double talk that is difficult to decipher, Paul actually uses two different words in Greek, heteros and allos. The former suggests "of a different kind" while the latter refers to something "of the same kind." Paul says that the gospel the Judaizers were peddling was one "of a different kind," and thus not similar to the one preached by the apostles. To get such distinctions in a translation is difficult without resorting to a whole sentence just to translate one word or short phrase into the English.

In Galatians, by reading the KJV, one would conclude that the term "heathen" (Gal. 3:8) and the word "Gentiles" (verse 14) are two different words in the Greek, but not so. The same Greek term in both verses is one and the same: *ta ethne*. It is certainly helpful to know this fact, is it not? Guy Woods points out that in Romans 3:2-3, the root word for faith is used four times, yet the King James translators translated it by four different words "committed, believe, unbelief, and faith." That Paul was emphasizing a play on words is obvious, yet we can totally miss that point in translation.

Whether a word in the original language is past tense or present tense helps in our understanding of what the writer is saying. Furthermore, what kind of past tense is referred to: aorist, perfect, or imperfect? Was the action in the past tense continuous or point action?

With these introductory remarks, we continue what we started in Volume 1 of Gems from the Greek, and hope that by it our readers might be better equipped to *handle aright the word of truth*" (2 Tim. 2:15).

Wayne Price M.A.

Table Of Contents

It's All Greek to Me	1
Order	5
Pass it on (2 Tim. 2:2)!	9
Perilous Porneia	12
Thelo	16
Sink Down into Your Ears	21
The First Day of Every Week	24
This and That	28
"…To Draw Away Disciples after Them"	31
When an Elder's Wife Dies	35
For – In Order to or Because of?	39
Forsaken by God	42
Keep that which is Entrusted to You	47
Having Access	50
Holiness – A Requirement?	53
Laud Him, All Ye People (Rom. 15:11)	56
Love and Shepherding	59
Laying on of Hands	62
No Elders After 1st Century?	65
No, Not to Eat	71

Rest with Us 74
Who did What? 78
"Go to Now" 81
Faithful Children 84
Dung (Phil. 3:8) 88
A Call to the Performance of a Task 91
Does the Holy Spirit Intercede for Us? 94
"Remission of Sins" Modifies which Verb in
Acts 2:38 97
Saved Through Water? 99
"Shall be 'Burned up' or 'Found'"? 103
The Use of Negatives in New Testament Greek 107
What does the Term Ekkleesia Mean? 113
Many Uses of the Present Tense 116
The Demoting of Christ #2 119
The Word 'For' in Acts 2:38 – 'In order to' or
'Because of'? 128
Does 1 Cor. 13 Refer to the Completion of the New
Testament Canon? 133
Old Man – New Man (Rom. 6:6; Eph. 4:22-24;
Col. 3:9-10) 136

Gems From The Greek

"It's All Greek to Me"

Other sayings, in addition to our title above, are quite common in our society. For example, you may have heard "I knew a little Greek once; he was about 5' 2" tall...," or "A little Greek hath made thee mad," et al. These are spoken in jest, but the following axiom is as serious as it can be: "The best commentary on the New Testament is the Greek New Testament." The more one studies the Greek N.T., the more he realizes this truism.

For example, oftentimes in the N.T., the Apostle Paul will use a "play on words" (i.e., a pun), but when it is translated into our English language, the reader may not even realize that he (Paul) is using the same word (or perhaps a form of the same word) in the very same verse. At times the translator will translate that double use of that word in the same context and will use the same English word both times to translate the original, thus helping the Bible student to see the pun, but when he translates the one Greek term by using two English synonyms, the Bible student may be oblivious to the fact that Paul is using the same word twice.

It is also true that knowing a little Greek can be dangerous! For example, the student who has taken only Greek 1, and decides that he needs no further study in this field, will have learned that the absence of the definite Greek article (the word "the" in front of a noun) may be rendered as "a" or "an." This is what your writer refers to when speaking of Jehovah's Witnesses and their treatment of the word Theos ("God") in John 1:1c. Their New World

Gems From The Greek

Translation of the Holy Scriptures has the following translation of that verse: "In [the] beginning the Word was, and the Word was with God, and the Word was a God." They argue that since the word Theos does not have the article in front of it, then it MUST be indefinite, hence "a" god! These translators should have taken Greek 2 and 3!

The fact they would have learned from further study is that the anarthrous Greek noun is not always translated as indefinite. If it has the article, it is definite, but if it lacks the article, it still may be definite, or it could be qualitative. So, in this instance (John 1:1c), the Jehovah's Witness translation stands as an example of a stunted growth in the Greek N.T.!

Alford informs us: "The omission of the article before Theos is not mere usage; it could not have been here expressed, whatever place the words might hold in the sentence. Ho logos een ho Theos would destroy the idea of the logos altogether. Theos must then be taken as implying God, in substance and essence, -not ho Theos, 'the Father,' in Person....as in sarx egeneto [John 1:14], sarx expresses that state into which the Divine Word entered by a definite act, so in Theos een, Theos expresses that essence which was His en archee: -that He was very God. So that this first verse might be connected this: the Logos was from eternity, -was with God (the Father), -and was Himself God."

Daniel Wallace (Greek Grammar Beyond the Basics, p. 266) writes that translating it as "a god", the NWT implies some form of polytheism, perhaps suggesting that the Word was merely a secondary god in a pantheon of deities. Also damaging to their argument that Theos (John 1:1c) does not have the article, they fail to mention that the identical construction is found elsewhere in this same chapter, but they do NOT translate it as "a god" on those occasions - why not? Their inconsistency suggests a theological bias on their part!

Furthermore, it has been pointed out that there are 282 occurrences of the anarthrous THEOS. At sixteen places NWT has either a god, god, gods or godly. Sixteen out of 282 means that the translators were faithful to their translation principle only 6% of the time.

Additionally, Wallace points out (p. 267) that "it is interesting that the New World Translation renders Theos as "a god" on the simplistic grounds that it lacks the article. This is surely an insufficient basis. (If that is a valid argument then) arche should be "a beginning" (1:1,2), zoee should be "a life" (1:4), para Theou should be "from a god" (1:6), Iwannees should be "a John" (1:6", Theon should be "a god" (:18), etc. Yet none of these other anarthrous nouns is rendered (by the NWT) with an indefinite article. One can only suspect strong theological bias in such a translation...Thus, contextually, and grammatically, it is highly improbable that the Logos could be "a god" according to John. Finally, the evangelist's own theology militates against this view, for there is an exalted Christology in the Fourth Gospel, to the point that Jesus Christ is identified as God (cf. 5:23; 8:58; 10:30; 20:28, etc.).

Gems From The Greek

So, is THEOS in John 1:1c indefinite, definite, or qualitative? Well, it is not indefinite; it might be definite, but is probably qualitative. Christ shared the essence of the Father, even though they differed in person. It is declaring the fact that Christ is deity, even though He is not the Father, thus the Word was God.

Gems From The Greek

Order

Word studies can be an interesting and enlightening pursuit, and even if a bit painstaking at times, it remains a worthwhile endeavor. The Greek word on which our study is to focus is taxis, meaning "order," and it is found ten times in the Greek New Testament.

The first writer to use the term is Luke, where he writes regarding Zacharias and his priestly duties at the temple: "*...while he executed the priest's office before God in the order of his course*" (Luke 1:8). That course is defined as the course of Abia (or Abijah), see verse 5. Ray Summers (Commentary on Luke, p. 25) states that "There were so many priests in the system at that time that they served in rotation by families, and even by divisions or ranks within the families." So, Luke informs us that this was in accordance to a fixed order or pattern. Similarly, we use the term to refer to a baseball manager turning in" the batting order" to the umpires prior to the start of a ballgame. Perhaps another term to describe it would be "taking turns" according to a fixed pattern. The NEB renders the prepositional phrase as "the turn of his division'; the Berkeley Version has "in the sequence of his series."

Secondly, In 1 Corinthians 14:40, Paul writes: "*Let all things be done decently and in order.*" The original states: "according to order." Church services at Corinth were getting "out of hand," and earlier in this same chapter, Paul had warned his readers that "*all things were to be done unto edifying*" (v. 26) but now reiterates the message in an even more forceful manner (v. 40). It appears that the

Gems From The Greek

exercising of spiritual gifts in the first century when the church met was a real problem (see verses 26-40) and was causing confusion instead of bringing about edification! Some order needed to be introduced in the exercise of such gifts. Incidentally this could be corrected by realizing that instead of a spiritual gift controlling the speaker, the speaker was to control his spiritual gift (v. 32). In the midst of chaos, confusion and disorder, a practice of establishing order was called for. Conclusion? Things were to be done "according to order." We would do well to remember this teaching today when modernists advocate randomness in worship. Unplanned worship services are haphazard and lacking in organization and structure. Yet some argue that such services are more spiritual, emotional, and meaningful. Such misguided folks need to read 1 Corinthians 14:37!

Thirdly, the Apostle Paul again used taxis, his second such usage of "order", in Col. 2:5: *"For though I be absent in the flesh, yet am I with you in the spirit, joying and beholding your order, and the stedfastness of your faith in Christ."* From Paul's vocabulary, the Holy Spirit inspired Paul to use a military metaphor "taxis," which referred to a keeping of the lines in order, or "staying in step." See also 2 Thessalonians 3:6 where Paul uses the word "disorderly" to describe a weak brother who is "out of step." Arndt/Gingrich (A Greek-English Lexicon of the New Testament, p. 119) states that the adverb ataktoos (located in 1 Clement 40:2) is used to describe "irregular religious services." Obviously, the opposite of orderly is disorderly.

Gems From The Greek

The remainder of the usages of taxis in the New Testament are all from the book of Hebrews, and all of them refer to Christ being a priest "*according to the order of Melchizedek.*" These references are as follows: Hebrews 5:6, 10; 6:20; 7:11 (twice), 17, 21. Note that the mere citation of the references to taxis is **according to the order** of the appearances of this word in our N.T.

Arndt/Gingrich (Ibid., p. 811) suggests that these "refer not only to a higher rank, but also to the entirely different nature of Melchizedek's priesthood, as compared with that of Aaron (7:11)." So, the idea of nature, quality manner, condition or appearance are uppermost in the mind of Paul when he quotes from Psalm 110:4.

The basic point of Hebrews 7:1-17 is to establish the relationship between Melchizedek and Christ. Notice that "(1) Neither Christ nor Melchizedek was of the Levitical tribe, yet both were priests; (2) both were superior to Abraham, (3) both were royal priests, i.e., they were both kings and priests, and (4) their priesthood were not obtained by ancestral relationships like that of the priests under the Levitical order. ..The statement that he was "without" father, mother, genealogy, etc. has reference to his official position, not to his physical being. He came suddenly into view, ...and vanished from the historical scene just as abruptly leaving behind him no details whatsoever of ancestry, descendants, father or mother,...circumstances of death" etc. Christ's priesthood was to be unchanging, unlike that Aaron. This would not be an order where taking turns serving as priest would continue; that was now history.

Gems From The Greek

"These omissions of details, by the Holy Spirit, through the writer of Hebrews, were designed, so the sacred text informs us, as indisputable evidence of the superiority of the priesthood of Christ to that of Levi (Guy N. Woods, Questions and Answers, pgs. 302-303). Hence, Christ's priesthood followed a fixed succession or "order" all right, but it was according to the order of Melchizedek, not that of Aaron!

Gems From The Greek

Pass It On (2 Tim. 2:2)!

In his charge to his son in the faith, Timothy (2 Tim. 1:2; 2:1), Paul urges him to pass on to other faithful men that which he learned from Paul himself. They would then be able to teach others also. Paul would not live forever, neither would Timothy.

Paul mentions that Timothy had heard the things Paul taught *"among many witnesses"* (v. 2 – KJV, NKJV, ASV). The Greek preposition used here by Paul is dia, and this term (when used with the genitive case in Greek) carries the meaning of "through." The RSV and Moffatt translate the expression "before many witnesses." Other versions render it as follows: "In the presence of" (NEB, NASV, NIV), "through many witnesses" (McCord), "by many witnesses" (Campbell, Living Oracles), "in public" (Jerusalem Bible), etc.

All are attempting to get at the meaning of the prepositional phrase "through" or "by means of." In his first letter to Timothy, Paul reminded Timothy that he (Timothy) had confessed the good confession "before many witnesses" but the preposition used there is not the same as here in 2 Timothy 2:2. In 1 Timothy 6:12, Paul uses the preposition enoopion "in the presence of."

Carl Spain writes that in 2 Tim. 2:2, "the preposition is 'with' or 'through.' It may be that Paul is speaking out of his experience of having witnesses called to testify concerning his teaching. In other words, Paul may be using witness (marturos) in a legal sense (cf. Matt. 26:65; Acts 6:13, 7:58; 2 Cor. 13:1; 1 Tim. 5:19). It may carry something of the same import as his words to the Thessalonians, 'while we preached to you the gospel of God. You are witnesses, and God also, how holy, and righteous and blameless was our behavior'" (1 Thess. 2:9b, 10) – The Letters of Paul to Timothy and Titus, <u>The Living Word Commentary</u>, Vol. 14, p. 123.

A second interesting word in this context is the verb "*commit*" (v.2, KJV). Timothy was to commit or entrust (2 aorist imperative from <u>paratitheemi</u>). Timothy was commanded to entrust or "deposit" this gospel with faithful men who could be counted on to entrust it to others. In a previous article, it was pointed out that the noun form of this word with the imperative of <u>phulasso</u>, meaning "to guard or protect the deposit" was used in 1 Timothy 6:20. Then in this second letter, Paul again uses the word in chapter one, verse 14 where he admonishes Timothy guard the good deposit (i.e., the gospel) and to do so by means of the Holy Spirit which dwelt in him, probably a reference to exercising the miraculous gift of discerning of spirits. The gospel would continue to need guarding after it was initially given by inspiration, until it was finally put in writing, hence being vouchsafed by this miraculous gift of the first century church.

Of course, after Timothy had carried out this obligation of delivering the gospel to faithful men, and the miraculous age had passed, no such gifts were needed any longer. Paul often referred to the written word (Col. 4:16; Eph. 3:3,4) as did John (John 21:24,25). Now we are to "*contend earnestly for the faith **once delivered***" as stated in Jude 3.

Men to whom the gospel was deposited must be trustworthy. It would appear that Timothy was to exercise judgment as to their being trustworthy or reliable. They were to be believers (i.e. Christians) **and** they were to be people of character, or reliable.

Much heartache and disappointment arise from those whom we thought at one time met these qualifications, but regarding whom we made a bad judgment call. Earlier Demas was evidently considered by Paul to be reliable (Col. 4:14; Philemon 24) but later was a disappointment to him (2 Tim. 4:10). What a joy it is, on the other hand, to know that your *"children walk in the truth"* (3 John 4).

The world out there has all kinds of people in it: atheists, skeptics, agnostics, as well as those who are just plain irreligious. They are considered to be good folks, when it comes to issues of paying their bills, but pertaining to important matters, it would seem they do not have a "religious bone" in their body. Paul perhaps includes all these under one word *"earthly."* In Philippians 3:19, he described some of his first century counterparts as those who *"mind earthly things,"* i.e. their minds on set on earthly matters. Paul instructed or first century brethren at Colossae to set *"their affection on things above, not on things on the earth"* (Col. 3:2) and the Master Teacher put it well when He said: *"Lay not up for yourselves treasures upon the earth, where moth and rust doeth corrupt, and where thieves break through and steal"* (Matt. 6:19).

Gems From The Greek

Perilous Porneia

The Greek noun porneia is found 26 times in the New Testament and is usually associated with evil, uncleanness, wickedness, and/or sexual sin. In addition to well-known passages in the N.T. such as Matt. 5:32; 19:9, et al., Christians are instructed to "*flee fornication*" (1 Cor. 6:13), "*avoid fornication*" (1 Cor. 7:2), and to "*let it not once be named among you, as becometh saints*" (Eph. 5:3).

Other terms in the same family of words are: the verb porneuoo = commit fornication, pornee = harlot, pornos = male prostitute, fornicator. All of these are also found in the N.T. However, fornication is also used figuratively in our Bibles portraying apostasy from God, sometimes to refer to practicing idolatry, and to describe governmental authorities in their hostility toward Christianity. Notice that the word "whore" is used as a symbol of opposing God (Rev. 17:5, 15ff.).

Recently an article was called to the attention of this writer that stated that *ekporneuoo* (Jude 7) "is not homosexuality, but UNRESTRAINED LUST." It goes on to argue that in the Septuagint (where it is found 47 times), it is limited to (1) prostitution, (2) playing the whore, and (3) idolatry. It argues that this lust is "above and beyond" the desire of a man for a woman. It is lust without boundaries or restraint. Question: Are we to now assume that a lesser amount of lust is alright, just as long as it is not excessive, and/or does not include homosexuality?

Gems From The Greek

We want to focus on these unusual comments on Jude 7 for the remainder of this article you now hold in your hand.

Is the use of the word fornication in Jude 7 erroneous? Obviously, it includes homosexuality, whether it is consensual or not. In the past, it has been argued that what happened and was condemned that day at Sodom, was not homosexuality but rather the sin was not showing hospitality (Gen. 19:1-11). I.e., they want you to believe that what happened at Sodom was not sodomy, but a lack of friendliness.

They argue that what happened in Sodom included more than just males ("all the people" - Gen. 19:4). Hence, in their view, the word <u>ekporneuoo</u> includes women also, and is describing illegitimate sexual activity, but not a condemnation of sodomy at all. That's quite a rewrite from what the text is teaching. The warning of not wresting the Scriptures to one's own destruction (2 Pet. 3:16) comes to mind.

The Bible says "*the men of the city, even the men of Sodom*" surrounded the house of Lot. Twice using the word "men" should settle the issue, but that is not sufficient for those with an agenda to push. So, they bring up verse 4 which says, "*all the people from every quarter.*" Aha, they argue, that has to include women also since it says, "all the people." We ask: "Why bring up women in this discussion? The writer of Genesis is merely describing the crowd of men there that day. Leupold (<u>Exposition of Genesis</u>, Vol. 1, p. 558) declares: "The expression, 'men of Sodom,' is no gloss (Kit. etc.), but it rather seems to have

Gems From The Greek

been a proverbial designation for outstanding exponents of the vice of sodomy, even while the city yet stood. Therefore, we have rendered it "men of Sodom that they were." Not only were they men of Sodom, they ranged from the young men to the old men, from every section of the town. "Hence the term 'all the people' describes the same men coming from throughout the town. If "all the people" means all women and children too in Gen. 19:4, then children and babies must have been included as receiving John's baptism since "all Judea" came to be baptized (Matt. 3:5-6). Obviously, "all the people" is an idiom that often means a large number of individuals, and that's what it refers to in Gen. 19:4 as well!

Furthermore, it is argued that what these Sodomites were lusting after was angelic beings of a different flesh. Peter (2 Pet. 2:6-10) does not use the word "strange" as did Jude, but it needs to be pointed out that "strange" can mean "unauthorized," according to Lev. 10:1, so there is no need to introduce the idea in Gen. 19:5 that the men of the city lusted after angelic flesh for a new type of experience! After all, even Lot himself never recognized these two travelers as angels until after they had smitten the Sodomites miraculously with blindness!

In regard to the verb <u>ekporneuoo</u>, remember that prepositions are often found in compounds added to the front of a verb. In such cases, the preposition (here in Jude 7 it is <u>ek</u> which is added to <u>porneuoo</u>). The idea of "out" is added to the meaning of the verb and enriched it with the idea of being intensive. These Sodomites were wholly given to their ungodly lifestyle.

Gems From The Greek

The noun porneia often corresponds to the English word "fornication," but it is an error to limit it to that meaning. The word had a broader scope and included sexual immorality" of various kinds (see Arndt-Gingrich Greek Lexicon, pp. 699-700). It says that it refers to "prostitution, unchastity, fornication, of **every kind of unlawful sexual intercourse** (emphasis mine, wp)...At times it is differentiated from moicheia ("adultery" - Matt. 15:19, etc.). On the other hand, moicheia appears as porneia (cf. Sir 23:23)...Of the sexual unfaithfulness of a married woman (Matt. 5:32; 19:9)."

As stated, the word porneia could be used for "adultery" (Sirach 23:22-23; probably Matthew 19:9), for "incest" (Testament of Reuben 1:6; 1 Cor. 5:1), and for "homosexuality," or "sodomy" (Testament of Benjamin 9:1). This note from the pen of Everett Ferguson makes it quite clear that porneia has a much broader usage than some would give it - and that it includes homosexuality, even in Jude 7!

It appears that we still have some Athenian type of folks with us today: "...*For all the Athenians and strangers which were there spent their time in nothing else, but either to tell, or to hear* **some new thing** [emphasis mine, wp]" (Acts 17:21).

Gems From The Greek

Thelo

As Bible students are aware, many original Greek words are translated into our English language by numerous synonyms, and even the King James Version often renders the same Greek word by different English equivalents. Perhaps this truth is as well represented by the Greek verb serving as the title of this article thelo as much as by any other original word which we might select.

This word, whose basic meaning is "to wish, desire, take pleasure in, be inclined or ready" is found over two hundred times in our New Testament. The King James translators used eighteen different words, such as *will, would, desire,* plus fifteen less frequent words in translating this fascinating Greek verb.[1] The burden of this short treatise is to focus on the problems caused by using the first two words (*will,* and *would*) in the rendering of this word into English.

Translating from one language into another is made more difficult when that target language (the English, let's say) uses a word which means more than one thing to its English readers. It is our misunderstanding of the *English* language rather than the Greek which causes many problems in Biblical interpretation.

Oftentimes in our English language, we use auxiliary verbs (or "helping" verbs) in forming a sentence: i.e., *am* going, *were* lost, *should* watch, etc. "*Be, do,* and *have* are the commonest auxiliaries; *can, may, shall, will, must, ought, should, would,* and *might* are frequently used as auxiliaries.[2] It is this very construction that sometimes causes the reader to misunderstand what the New Testament writer was saying, especially as it pertains to the use of the Greek verb thelo. In addition, the English words *would* and *will* can also show simple futurity which further complicates the problem for Bible students.

The Greek word thelo is *not* to be understood as *an auxiliary verb*, nor as expressing something that is to happen in the future, but rather as emphasizing "the will, or desire" to do a thing, much akin to the Greek word boulomai. This is the primary significance of the term. Places in these two categories where students might miss the point made by the inspired writers are listed below.

At the time when the King James Version was translated into English, no doubt the common folk understood the terms "will" and "would" to be expressing "intent and/or desire," but many people in the world today perceive these words to mean something else. Examples of where some might erroneously believe that the **auxiliary verb** is being used include the following:

Matthew 18:30 – Instead of "would not," we should understand it to be saying, "**was not inclined**" or "did not desire" to be patient.

Matthew 23:37 – Instead of understanding our Lord to merely be saying that people "would not" come, we need to realize he was addressing their mindset; they just **did not desire** to come to Him.

2 Thess. 3:10 – "would not" work is best understood as meaning these lazy persons just

did not desire to work.

Passages where some students might think that simple futurity is being expressed (instead of the will to do something) are as follows:

Matthew 20:26,27 – Instead of saying "Whosoever will be great…(i.e., sometime in the future), Jesus stresses the desire or wish that a person has to be great. To better understand what Jesus emphasizes, we need to realize that He is saying "Whosoever **wishes** (desires, et al.) to be great among you…" A number of the new versions available clear up this problem caused by the English reader's use of "will" as an auxiliary verb.

In John 5:38-40, Jesus challenges the Jews to search the Scriptures, for the Scriptures testified of Him, and yet they refused to accept the import of their own Scriptures! Amazing! Then in verse 40, He gives the reason why this is the case. "Ye *will not* come to me , that ye might have life." This is not simply the future tense of the verb "come," far from it. The Greek literally says: "you do not desire to come", with the words "to come" being the infinitive, not the finite verb. Again, they just did not desire (did not wish) to come to Christ!

In Acts 17:18, some of the Epicurean and Stoic philosophers were not asking "what will this babbler say?" but rather what does he "**desire** to say." Other terms such as **wish**, **want**, et al. do a fine job in expressing the concept of desire inherent within the Greek verb.

Gems From The Greek

Realizing this simple point surely makes the text "come alive" for the Bible student.

A few other passages illustrating this point include:

1 Cor. 7:39 "to be married to whom she will" is better understood "to whom she **desires**…"

Gal. 1:7 is not simply saying that some "would pervert the gospel of Christ" but instead informs us that they **wish** to pervert the gospel.

In 1 Tim. 2:4, the point emphasized is not that God "will have all men to be saved" (i.e., future tense), but that God "**desires**" all men to be saved.

Finally, in Rev. 22:17 we have the articular use of the participle, and our word <u>thelo</u> is that participle, used as a noun since it has the article in front of it. Note that the text says, "Whosoever will, let him take the water of life freely." Again, this is not using the word "will" as an auxiliary verb modifying "take," but rather this is our word <u>thelo</u>. Literally, the text reads "the one desiring (or the one who wishes), let him take the water of life freely."

Numerous other examples could be cited, but these few references should suffice to illustrate the point. Some people have a problem understanding the use of "will, would" in our English language, especially as it relates to the Greek word <u>thelo</u>.

Gems From The Greek

It is hoped this short study will prove beneficial in the study of the English Bible, especially as it relates to the meaning of the original verb thelo.

Endnotes:

[1]Winter, Ralph, The Word Study Concordance (Tyndale House Publishers, Inc., 1978), pp. 362-63.

[2]Perrin, Robert, Writer's Guide, and Index to English (Scott, Foresman and Company, 1959), p. 435.

Gems From The Greek

"Sink Down Into Your Ears"

In Luke 9:44, the wording employed by the King James Version translators in rendering the verb used in our title is vivid one indeed. The verb is <u>titheemi</u>, and it is quite common in the New Testament (found some ninety-six times). Its meaning is "to place, put, lay" etc. It would appear that the more colorful use of the term "sink down" came from the context, and not the primary significance of the Greek verb itself. A literal translation of this would be "Put ye these words into your ears."

Technically, the command given by our Lord is described as 2nd aorist imperative, 2nd person plural and in the middle voice. His disciples were having difficulty in understanding His prophecy that "*The Son of man must suffer many things and be rejected of the elders and chief priests and scribes, and be slain, and be raised the third day*" (Luke 9:22). Some time had passed between verse 22 and verse 44 (see verses 28 and 37). They should not permit the Lord's acts of kindness, His miracles, etc. (verses 38-40) to detract from His upcoming death, burial and resurrection! Perhaps their difficulty with His comments was due to the fact that they just could not conceive of their Messiah being treated in such a fashion. Yes, Isaiah 53, given some 700+ years earlier, should have made the Lord's prediction more palatable, but this was not the only time they had such difficulty (see Luke 2:50; Luke 18:34, et al.). This evidently did not fit into their scheme of things, even though it fit perfectly into God's scheme of redemption (Luke 24:44-47). Even now, when a teacher sees that his students appear to be having difficulty in understanding what he (the teacher) meant, he might use the everyday figurative expression, "Now let this sink in" and then slowly repeat what he said earlier.

In Mark 9:31-33, we see another issue that drew His disciples' attention away from the important matter of Christ on Calvary toward one that was divisive and petty. Jesus asked them: *"What was it that ye disputed among yourselves by the way?"* (v. 33). Mark informs us exactly what that discussion was all about! After Jesus asked them the question, they evidently hesitated to answer: *"But they held their peace: for by the way they had disputed among themselves, who should be the greatest"* (v. 34). Of course, Jesus already knew what they were thinking (Luke 9:47), but asked the question anyway, putting them on the spot. Instead of being concerned about His death and resurrection, they had been arguing about where they ranked as disciples of the Lord. The point we want to make in this article is that when Christians fight and quarrel among themselves, the very reason for their existence as His disciples is diminished (Luke 19:10). Perhaps this issue of "who was the greatest?" was part of the reason why His disciples had a problem in understanding the significance of what the Lord was saying (Mark 9:32).

We mentioned above that the verb <u>titheemi</u> is often translated as "place, put or lay," but these renderings do not exhaust the variety of terms used in translating this verb. To illustrate this fact, we offer the following few examples:

This verb is sometimes translated as "appoint" (Matt. 24:51, Luke 12:46) but translated "ordained" in John

Gems From The Greek

15:16; "appointed" (1 Thess. 5:9). Paul wrote that he was "ordained a preacher" (1 Tim. 2:7) and "appointed a preacher" (2 Tim. 1:11) as found in the KJV. Interestingly enough, in 1 Tim. 1:12, Paul is pictured as declaring that Christ had "put" him into the ministry. All of these last three references by Paul are translated by the KJV from the same Greek verb *titheemi*! This illustrates that the KJV translators had no problems with translating the same Greek verb with different synonyms into the target language - English (in 1611 A.D.)

Our Greek verb is also used in Luke 21:14, where it is translated as "settle." Jesus warns His disciples that they will be hauled into court, and He gives them instructions on HOW handle the situation. He instructs them to not prepare speeches beforehand, because in that hour when they are allowed to speak in their own defense, Christ Himself would give them what they were to say (v. 15). Robertson writes: "It is the preparation for the speech of defence (apology) that Jesus here forbids, not the preparation of a sermon (Word Pictures, Vol. 2, p. 258).

Finally, the word is also translated as "kneeling down" (literally having placed one's knee) in Acts 7:60, 9:40, 20:36 and 21:5. Numerous references could be cited where this verb is cited by the KJV translators with other types of activities. Ananias was said to have "conceived" in his heart to lie unto God (Acts 5:4); i.e. Ananias placed such a thought in his own heart! The truth is, by just reading from one English translation alone, we probably would never realize that all of these different English verbs actually translate the one same Greek verb titheemi!

Gems From The Greek

The First Day of Every Week?

In 1 Corinthians 16:2, the apostle Paul writes these familiar words: "*Upon the first day of the week let every one of you lay by him in store, as God hath prospered him, that there be no gatherings when I come.*" This verse, when used to show the necessity of meeting with the saints every Lord's Day, is often challenged with the following retort: "It does not say **every** first day of the week."

This argument is countered with the facts regarding the Sabbath Day enactment, and is then paralleled with Acts 20:7, Hebrews 10:25, etc., showing that the Lord did not say "every" Sabbath when giving the Ten Commandments (Exodus 20:8) either, yet the Israelites understood the positively stated command as meaning "every." During the wilderness wanderings, a certain individual had gathered sticks on the Sabbath Day, a clear violation of the fourth commandment of the Decalogue. Numbers 15:32-36 records the command that he be stoned to death outside the camp. One could almost hear modern man, had he been the one guilty of disregarding the Sabbath law shouting, "But God did not say **every** Sabbath," even as the stones sailed toward his head.

Such examples are forceful, logical, and irrefutable. It needs to be pointed out however that the basic argument which maintains that "God did not say every first day of the week" is just not true. The fact is that this is exactly what the apostle Paul records as being the Lord's commandment (1 Corinthians 14:37) regarding the frequency of the assembly (Hebrews 10:25; 1 Corinthians 16:2).

Gems From The Greek

The basic meaning of the Greek preposition kata, when not found in composition with other words, is "down," but one of its resultant meanings (when used with the accusative case) signifies "down along," "according to," etc. Hence, when this Greek preposition is followed by a direct object in the accusative case, we may have what is called the distributive usage of kata. This particular construction is found quite often in our New Testaments, especially in the writings of Luke.

It is not difficult to see how that "down along the cities" evolved into the idea of "every" city. The phrase "down along the synagogues" meant "from synagogue to synagogue," or "every synagogue." The phrase "down along the years" could be translated "year by year," "annually" or "every year."

This writer has divided the occurrences of the distributive used of kata into two groups, one dealing with TIME and the other dealing with PLACE. These two lists are by no means intended to be exhaustive, but rather illustrative. All citations are from the King James Version.

As related to the concept of TIME, the distributive use of kata is variously translated, with the idea of "each" or "every" either inherent within the meaning of the translation or else specifically stated. Note these examples relating to the time element:

Matthew 26:55 "I sat *daily* with you"

Luke 2:41 "his parents went to Jerusalem *every* year"

Luke 16:19 "rich man...fared sumptuously *every* year"

Gems From The Greek

Luke 19:47 "he taught *daily* in the temple"

Luke 22:53 "I was *daily* with you"

Acts 2:46 "continuing *daily* with one accord"

Acts 2:47 "Lord added to the church *daily*"

Acts 3:2 "whom they laid *daily*"

Acts 16:5 "increased in number *daily*"

Acts 17:11 "searched the scriptures *daily*"

1 Corinthians 15:31 "I die *daily*"

1 Corinthians 16:2 "? ? ? ? ?"

2 Corinthians 11:28 "that which cometh upon me *daily*"

     Regarding the idea of PLACE, the following examples show how the King James translators rendered this distributive use of <u>kata</u>:

Luke 8:1 "he went throughout *every* city"

Luke 8:4 "out of *every* city"

John 21:25 "if they should be written *every*one"

Acts 15:21 "*every* city them that preach him"

Acts 20:23 "*every* city"

Acts 22:19 "*every* synagogue"

Ephesians 5:33 "let *every* one of you ...love his wife"

Titus 1:5 "ordain elders in *every* city"

Gems From The Greek

All of the above citations illustrate that the translators of the King James New Testament, on numerous occasions, rendered this distributive <u>kata</u> usage as "every." Our question is why did they not do so in 1 Corinthians 16:2? Would not consistency demand that it be translated the same here as elsewhere in the King James Version?

The answer to the question found in the title of this paper is a resounding "YES." First Corinthians 16:2 ought to read: "every first day of the week" and the word "every" need not be put in italics either, for the original language in which the New Testament was written contains the idea of "each" or "every" in this verse also.

Gems From The Greek

This and That

2 Timothy 2:25b-26 (KJV, Living Oracles) says: "…if God peradventure will give them repentance to the acknowledging of the truth; and that they may recover themselves out of the snare of the devil, who are taken captive by him at his will."

The following versions illustrate their efforts at translating this passage. "Taken captive by him to do his will" (NJKV, NASV,RSV, NIV). Also having both demonstratives (autou and ekeinou) to refer to the devil but rendering it a bit differently are the following examples: "(devil) captured them for his purpose" (McCord's New Testament), and "the devil caught them and kept them enslaved" (New Jerusalem Bible). However, it must be noted that the RSV and the NEB both have footnotes which inform the reader that it is possible that it is "God's will" that is in focus in verse 26, not the devil's. Other versions, instead of relegating to the footnotes the possibility of this being God's will, go ahead and so translate it into their text. For example, Phillip's translation says: "they may come to their senses and be rescued from the snare of the devil by the servant of the Lord and set to work for God's purposes." The Living Bible gives this interesting rendering: "Then they will come to their senses and escape from Satan's trap of slavery to sin which he uses to catch them whenever he likes, and then they can begin doing the will of God." The ASV's translation is as follows: "if peradventure God may give them repentance unto the knowledge of the truth, and they may recover themselves out of the snare of the devil, having been taken captive by

Gems From The Greek

him unto his will." But its (the ASV's footnotes) inform us: "or by him, unto the will of God…Gr. By him, unto the will of him. In the Greek the two pronouns are different."

This section, admittedly difficult to interpret, is rendered differently by various Bible versions as illustrated above, as they focus on who it was that took captives, and by whose will was it done. Robertson states the difficulty well when he says "this difficult phrase is understood variously. One way is to take both demonstrative pronouns (autou and ekeinou) to refer to the devil. Another way (2) is to take both of them to refer to God. Another way (3) is to take autou of the devil and ekeinou, of God (Robertson, A.T., Word Pictures in the New Testament, Vol. 4, p. 622).

Summers sums up the use of demonstrative pronouns this way. "There are two demonstrative pronouns in Greek. The near demonstrative (outos) points out something near at hand; the remote demonstrative points out something further removed (ekeinos)" (Summers, Ray, Essentials of New Testament Greek, p. 47). It should be noted that this concept relates not only to "space" or "location," but also to nearness or distance in a literary context. To illustrate, if I were pointing out to you a book in my hand, I would say "this book" but if I were referring to a book across the room, I would say "that book." This has to do with my actual physical location in relation to the book I am discussing with you. But the demonstrative also is used to describe that which is nearer or more distant "in thought" and/or "in written material" as well, and 2 Tim. 2:25-26 may well be a good example of the latter.

Gems From The Greek

The pronouns in question are outos (this one), and ekeinos (that one), but these demonstratives are also used as emphatic personal pronouns as well, and hence may be rendered as "he." When bringing this usage over into English, it may cause problems, since depending upon the case, i.e. nominative or objective, outos (this one) is often translated as "he" or "him", but ekeinos (that one) may also be translated as "he" or "him."

Look at the illustration below:

The last phrase "who are taken captive by him at his will," literally says "who are taken captive by him" ('this one' nearer in the context: i.e., Satan) at his ('that one' more remote in the context: God) will." Paul states that men, through repentance, might recover their sobriety of mind, thereby extricating themselves from the devil's trap, and return "unto" (Greek is eis) the will of God.

With this conclusion Robertson would agree, for after stating the three possibilities of interpreting this phrase (see the third paragraph of this treatise), Robertson says regarding the third interpretation, i.e., taking autou to refer to Satan, and ekeinou to refer to God), that it "is probably best, 'taken captive by the devil' that they may come back to soberness to do the will of God" (Ibid.).

Gems From The Greek

"...To Draw Away Disciples After Them" (Acts 20:30)

The Apostle Paul warned the elders of the church in Ephesus that sometime in their future, men would begin to speak misleading things in an effort to get disciples there in Ephesus to break away and follow after them (NEB - Acts 20:30). "To draw away" comes from the word spao = "to draw or pull" with the prefix "apo" attached to the front of that verb, meaning "from, or out of." The same word is used in Matthew 26:51 when describing Peter **drawing out** his sword and cutting off the ear of the high priest's servant, Malchus (John 18:10). This literal use of the term obviously has a figurative use in Acts 20:30 where drawing away the disciples is explained by Arndt/Gingrich Lexicon (p. 97) equaling "and thereby alienate them."

Probably it would be false doctrine they were peddling, or perhaps it would simply be a distortion (or spin made) of truth, but whatever it was, it deserved to be watched carefully. Notice that this effort to draw away disciples and make them followers of themselves could originate (or come from) among the leaders of the church themselves!

This warning not only included watching those outside the body of Christ (v. 29) but "*also of your own selves*" (v. 30 - KJV). They needed to be watchful - i.e., both externally and internally they needed to be on guard. Much of the time people (here "the flock") are less attuned to facts than they are to emotion!

Gems From The Greek

Notice that Paul declares that his primary interest was in the salvation of their souls (vss. 31-32), not financial remuneration! In fact, he bluntly states: "*I have coveted no man's silver, or gold, or apparel*" (v. 33). Of course, they might put their own spin on things in an effort to make Paul look bad, an effort which did take place as we see in the following paragraph.

Paul wrote the church in Philippi that "*Some indeed preach Christ even of envy and strife; and some also of good will: The one preach Christ of contention, not sincerely, supposing to add affliction to my bonds: But the other love, knowing that I am set for the defence of the gospel*" (Phil. 1:15-17).

Hence, we are dealing with the subject of motives, that is, **WHY people do what they do**! Paul declares that some were intentionally trying to hurt him personally, i.e. "*adding afflicting to my bonds*" even while preaching Christ! He also states that such efforts are not done "sincerely" (v. 16), hence they were done for the wrong motive.

Sometimes our motives are apparent to others, but sometimes the real motive may be hidden. That which causes a person to act in a certain way may range from thirst for power, to simple altruism, egotism, desire for money, hurt feelings, tradition, security, and a host of other things.

Possibly our motives are not so obvious, even to ourselves, due to self-deception. Certainly, the things we do (our actions themselves) will be considered regarding

Gems From The Greek

our status on the Judgment Day (2 Cor. 5:10), but surely our motives behind what we do are also very important (see Matt. 6:1-18). In fact, motives can be traced back to near the beginning of mankind here on this earth. John writes: *"For this is the message that ye heard from the beginning, that we should love one another. Not as Cain, who was of that wicked one, and slew his brother, And wherefore slew he him? Because his own works were evil, and his brother's righteous"* (1 John 3:11-12). Jealousy, disobedience, and unrighteousness were all involved in Cain's response to God's acceptance of Abel's obedience to God. Perhaps Cain's quick reaction was due to emotion (feeling slighted) and he acted not according to the facts and thinking things through, but rather due to unbridled, raw emotion (his feelings were hurt, and he lashed out at his brother), i.e. he was "getting even."

The children of Ammon attributed the wrong motive to King David In 2 Sam. 10:2-3. David was simply performing a kind deed to Hanun (v. 2), but others looked for an ulterior motive to make David look bad and charged David with trying to spy out the city and destroy it. It was not true, but what difference did that make, their minds were made up, and to them, David was the bad guy.

On another occasion, Jehoram, the king of Israel, had difficulty accepting things at their face value when the king of Syria made a request of him. The Syrian king wrote Jehoram, accompanied by silver and gold, and asked that his servant Naaman be healed of his leprosy. But the king of Israel accused the Syrian king of trying to cause a quarrel. He misjudged his motives, caused a misunderstanding, and Elisha stepped in and remedied the potential problem. He said: "*Wherefore hast thou rent thy clothes? let him (*Naaman the leper*) come now to me, and he shall know that there is a prophet in Israel*" (2 Kgs. 5:5-8). About the only exercise some folks get is "jumping to conclusions," attributing motives to others which are erroneous.

In reference to motives which people might have for doing things, suffice it to say that all of us need to "*let (y)our behavior be as it becometh the gospel of Christ*" (v. 27).

Gems From The Greek

"When An Elder's Wife Dies"

The specific point discussed in this article relates to an elder's situation when his wife passes away. Is he qualified to be an elder a moment before she leaves this earth, but unqualified a moment after?

The key references being addressed are 1 Timothy 3:1-7 and Titus 1:5-9. These qualifications given by the inspired Paul are to be applied to prospective elders, i.e. those who are being considered for the eldership. This is obvious when it is kept in context. Timothy is told that "*If a man desires the office of a bishop, he desires a good work,*" signifying the man is not yet an elder. He desires to be, and he can be if he meets the qualifications listed and is appointed. But he is not yet an elder.

One individual wrote: "Does the death of the wife of the elder disqualify him as an elder?" He answered his own question: "Yes." The argument given is that Titus 1:6, Paul says "*If anyone **be** the husband of one wife*" is what Paul wrote and since the present tense verb (is - estin) is used, it shows that a man who serves as an elder must progressively, at every moment, have a wife who is living.

But wait a moment! The previous verse declares: "*For this cause left I thee in Crete, that thou shouldest set in order the things that are wanting, and ordain elders in every city, as I had appointed thee*" (Titus 1:5). At that point, they had no elders, and Titus was sent there to take care of that matter and appoint qualified men as elders. Thus, both of these passages (1 Tim 3 and Titus 1) are describing men who are not yet elders, so Paul is discussing

the process of making elders, the appointment of elders, and not making reference to tragedies which may occur later on in the life of an elder!

Occasionally some will cite Romans 7:1-4 to show that an elder in the church ceases to be qualified to serve in that capacity whenever his wife dies. The problem with such argumentation is that it employs the age-old habit of disregarding the context! Paul is using the marriage relationship to illustrate that once a person's companion dies, he/she is free from the law since death abrogates legal bonds. He then applies this fact, which his readers understood quite well, to **being freed from the Law of Moses**. The fact is that no one living today has ever been under the Law of Moses, and furthermore Paul never even hinted that this example of Romans 7 should be applied to disqualify an elder from continuing to serve as an elder were his wife to die!

But it is true that tragic accidents can happen in the lives of any of us. Yes, an elder must meet the qualification of being "*the husband of one wife*" but his wife might die in a tragic car accident, or die from cancer ravaging her body, with such events being totally beyond his control. He's still the same man, with all the character traits he possessed earlier when appointed an elder, but his wife just died!

Is he now unqualified to serve any longer in that capacity? Paul does not even address such a situation!

Paul also states, when referring to the elder appointment situation, that the candidate must have "*faithful children*" (Titus 1:6; 1 Tim. 3:4-5). If it be the case that he has a 15-year-old girl, and a 17-year-old year old son, both faithful Christians, and after having been appointed an elder, his two teenagers die in a horrible car accident, both at the same time, is the elder no longer qualified because now he does not have (present tense) children? What if his wife and two children all die in the same accident? Is it the case that he could be (and was) an elder yesterday, but no longer today, due to these tragic deaths in his family? Another tragic possibility is that his children might die in a tornado, similar to what Job experienced (Job 1:18-19). Since he longer has children, is he disqualified as an elder?

A number of years ago, an elder had reared faithful children and both now had their own Christian homes. But then, an unplanned blessing occurred in the lives of this elder and his wife! They had another child, their first in about twenty years! Some folks thought he needed to resign, since this new baby was not a Christian yet! We must guard against forcing our opinions on others as if they were equal to Bible facts.

One has written: "What should the elder do in case his wife dies? Should he resign the eldership the next Sunday? Some have so affirmed but I am not of this number. When initially appointed he had the one wife and met with signal success the possession of that qualification. He may choose to resign and that is his prerogative. However, in my judgment, **the Scriptures do not demand that he do so**. Within in a year or two he may well remarry, and his second wife may enable him to do all or even more than he did when with his first companion.

Gems From The Greek

Even if he chooses never to remarry, he may still serve with efficiency in the eldership the rest of his active life. He still has in his background the necessary experience within the family framework to make successful his efficiency in the realm of the service that elders render..."

Not only was Peter an apostle, he was also a family man. He had a wife (Matt. 8:14) and children (1 Pet. 5:1). The latter reference informs us that he was an elder, thus showing that he had met two of the qualifications spelled out in Titus 1:6; being married and having children! But according to the interpretation of some brethren, the moment Peter's wife died (if she preceded him in death), he could no longer serve as an elder, since he was no longer "the husband of one wife." We might as well go another step further (since we are now assuming she preceded him in death) and declare that the moment that all of his children died, he likewise would have to resign as an elder, since he no longer had "faithful children."

The character traits still describe who he is, regardless of what might happen to his wife in a car accident. Losing such traits of character may disqualify him, but the death of his children, the death of his wife, or **things over which he has no control** are in a different category, not disqualifying him as an elder. The idea of an elder resigning is not even a part of the context penned by the apostle Paul in these verses, and to divide churches over such a personal interpretation is to make a tragic event even worse!

Gems From The Greek

For – In Order to or Because of?

Many of our Baptist preacher friends use the old argument that the Greek preposition (eis in Acts 2:38) is causal, and therefore it should be translated "because." The argument is that one is baptized BECAUSE his sins have already been remitted. Of course, if that were a valid argument, then it would necessarily be true also as it relates to repentance, for both repentance and baptism sustain the same relationship to the preposition eis. That would mean one repents because his sins have already been remitted!!! Just because the **English** word "for" has many usages, and "because" happens to be one of them, that does not mean the **Greek** word "eis" has such a meaning (Matt. 12:41, and a couple of others that are sometimes claimed to have such a use notwithstanding)!

However, just a quick check on the preposition eis shows that there is no such thing as a "causal" eis, in all of Koine Greek, whether Biblical or non-Biblical! The word is found 1773 times in the New Testament. By itself eis does not mean "into," "unto," or "towards," but that is the resultant idea when used with the accusative case. Eis is always prospective, never retrospective (i.e., because of), especially following verbs of motion.

J.R. Mantey admitted that none of the Greek lexicons translate eis as causal, so he and H.E. Dana made their own grammar which included it (H.E. Dana and J.R. Mantey, <u>A Manual Grammar of the Greek New Testament</u>, (New York: The MacMillan Company), 1957, pp. 103-104!!!

Gems From The Greek

However, when he presented his erroneous theory in the prestigious Journal of Biblical Literature, he was thoroughly spanked by one Ralph Marcus, who had no theological axe to grind, or religious bias to promote, as did Mantey. They exchanged a number of articles via the JBL, and Mantey searched for non-Biblical references to back up his hypothetical causal *eis* idea in extra-Biblical literature.

Marcus' conclusion? "...if, therefore, Prof. Mantey is right in his interpretation of various New Testament passages on baptism and repentance and the remission of sins, he is right for reasons that are **non-linguistic**." Perhaps that is what Mantey himself was getting at when he said that "one can interpret it (*eis*) according to his theology" (J.R. Mantey, "On Causal *Eis* Again," Journal of Biblical Literature, December 1951), p. 309). In other words, linguistics gives no evidence for a causal *eis*, but perhaps theological bias might!

In fact, even A.T. Robertson made a similar revealing admission: "After all is done, instances remain where syntax cannot say the last word, where theological bias will inevitably determine how one interprets the Greek idiom...So in Ac. 2:38 *eis* does not itself express design (see Mt. 12:41), but it may be so used. When the grammarian has finished, the theologian steps in, and sometimes before the grammarian is through" (A Grammar of the Greek N.T., p. 389). The fact is *eis* plus the accusative does express design, in order to obtain, etc., and Robertson is guilty of doing the very thing he mentions (allowing his theological bias to have supremacy over the grammar and syntax).

James W. Willmarth, a Baptist himself, said it well, although he allows his prejudicial language to be injected into his conclusion: "We are gravely told that if we render eis in Acts 2:38 'in order to secure,' we give up the battle and must forthwith become Campbellites; whereas if we translate it 'on account of," it will yet be possible for us to remain Baptists…When Campbellites translate 'in order to' in Acts 2:38, they translate correctly. Is a translation false because Campbellites endorse it" (Willmarth, Baptist Quarterly, July 1877, p. 304).

I prefer to rest my case on what the inspired Luke and Peter have to say rather than on what those who rely on theological bias might have to say. The fact remains that **the faith that saves is the faith that obeys** (see Rom. 1:5; 16:26; Acts 6:7; Heb.5:9); a disobedient faith saves no one (see James 2:17, 20, 24; John 12:42).

Gems From The Greek

Forsaken by God

Some people have serious problems with the idea that God actually forsook Christ when He endured the Calvary crucifixion. Various arguments are offered which themselves are suspect when compared with Biblical teaching on the subject.

To Whom Was Jesus Talking to in Matthew 27:46?

Some argue that Jesus was NOT speaking to God, the Father, because God had promised that He would "never forsake" us (Hebrews 13:5), but Jesus said that God was forsaking Him on the cross (Matt. 27:46). Hence, Jesus was speaking to the crowd that day, and not to His Father it is alleged.

However, the context of Heb. 13:5 is not even talking about the crucifixion of our Lord, but rather covetousness. Man is not to be covetous, but rather he ought to trust in God since God won't desert him. Yes, some in the crowd had deserted Jesus at Calvary, but He was not talking to them! Why? Because whoever it was, it was in the singular, not the plural. The word "God" is in the vocative case (the case of direct address) and it is **singular in number**, therefore proving that God is the One directly addressed, not members of the crowd around the cross that day. Additionally, the verb "forsaken" is singular, i.e. "**You**" abandoned, **not** "ye" have abandoned!

To argue that Jesus was using the expression "My God, My God" as a by-word or slang expression (as some suggest) for emphasis sake is to put Christ in the position of

Gems From The Greek

using flippant and profane terminology. The Bible states that the Lord God's name was not to be taken in vain (Deut 5:7-11). Christ certainly did not use this expression in this sacred name of "God" in a profane irreverent way. He was speaking to His Father using direct address and was not speaking euphemistically whatsoever.

Why Would Jesus Say That God Had Forsaken Him?

Somebody had forsaken Him, but why would Jesus say that God had done so (Matt. 27:46), and what actually is meant by the word "forsake?"

The verb "forsake" is from <u>egkataleipo</u>, found 8 times in the New Testament, and many more in the Old Testament. The basic meaning of the word is "to leave," sometimes in a good sense, and sometimes in a bad sense. If someone "left" you a thousand dollars, would that be good or bad? In this good sense, we have Romans 9:29 which says: *"Except the Lord of Sabaoth had **left** us a seed, we had been as Sodom and make like unto Gomorrah."* Here the term does not have the bad sense of "abandon." Obviously, that was good for mankind, even though it meant that Jesus Christ would be crucified, die, and be raised again the third day (1 Cor. 15:3-4). Hence the word can mean anything from "leave" to "leave survivors" as well as "forsake" or "leave behind," "leave in the straits, helpless, or in the lurch."

When a person visits a close friend in the hospital, and the patient asks :Why did you abandon me?" has he really been abandoned? Of course, not – his friend is right there in the same room with him and concerned about his health! But has he forsaken him? The patient may have felt that he had been LEFT in the lurch. This statement comes from the human side of our Lord, who was God/man for some 33 years while in human flesh.

God did NOT totally desert or forsake His Son forever, but only temporarily "left Him in the straits." Jesus Himself knew that He would be in the grave "*3 days and 3 nights*" (Matt. 12:40), He knew that "*He must be killed, and be raised again the 3rd day*" (Matt. 17:23;Luke 9:22,31; 24:7). He told His disciples in Mark 9:9-10 that He would rise from the dead [see also Luke 18:33, Luke 24:46, etc.].

Christ knew that He would be raised from the dead, so the term "forsake" cannot mean absolute desertion, but rather a temporary leaving, that God's plan for saving men could be implemented. God "gave His Son" and yet from Jesus' viewpoint He (Jesus) "laid it down" Himself (John 10:18). In fact, that is why He came to this earth, to die and give His life a ransom for many (Matt. 20:28). In His coming into the world for this very purpose, He said to His Father "*Sacrifice and offering Thou did not desire, but a body hast thou prepared me*" (Heb. 10:5), and then verse 10 says the purpose of giving Him a body was that He might give His life, and He knew that since He said "*I come to do thy will*, O God" (v. 9).

Since Christ knew His purpose for coming to earth, why did He day that God had "forsaken" Him (Matt. 27:46)?

Being LEFT to endure such sufferings, a person might thus address God. 2nd, there was probably something more than the physical agony alone that caused Him to utter this comment (in Matt. 27:46). Isaiah 53:4-5 says that *"he bore our griefs and carried our sorrows; that he was wounded for our transgressions and bruised for our iniquities; that the chastisement of our peace was laid on him; that by his stripes we are healed."* He died for us, *"bare our sins in his own body on the tree…"* (1 Pet. 2:24). God hates sin, yet Jesus Who knew no sin, was *"made sin for us..."* (2 Cor. 5:21). It was this that caused His intense suffering, and caused Him to say, *"My God, My God, why hast Thou forsaken Me?"* (Matt. 27:46).

Did Members of the Godhead Refer to Each Other as 'God'? Yes!

Jesus refers to His Father when He said: "O God' (Heb. 10:7,9). God, the Father, refers to Jesus when He said: "O God" (Heb. 1:8).

Since Christ Was Also 'God,' Can God Forsake Himself? No.

There are three (3) persons in the Godhead, all of which are deity! Yet because each is called God, does not mean that they no longer have an individual identity! One person of the Godhead (Jesus Christ) was addressing another person of the Godhead (God, the Father).

The Father **left** His Son to suffer on the cross for the sins of mankind. Christ had assumed human flesh: *"Forasmuch then as the children are partakers of flesh and blood, he also himself likewise took part of the same; that through death he might destroy him that had the power of death, that is, the devil"* (Heb. 2:14). At the time that Christ said *"Why hast Thou forsaken me?"* He was still in HUMAN form, feeling pure human emotion! He came to earth to complete God's plan for saving mankind, and that plan included dying for the sins of men (Heb. 2:9). He could have called for thousands of angels for deliverance, but had He done so, the plan of salvation for all mankind would have been thwarted (Matt. 26:53-54; Luke 24:26). He had prayed, *"Father, if Thou be willing, remove this cup from Me, nevertheless not my will, but thine, be done"* (Luke 22:42). Christ affirmed: *"For I came down from heaven not to do mine own will, but the will of Him that sent me"* (John 6:38). Truly, Christ came to do the Father's will, and in effect He made it His own.

Gems From The Greek

Keep That Which Is Entrusted To You

In the close of his first letter to Timothy, Paul charged his young son in the faith, to *"keep that which is committed to thy trust, avoiding profane and vain babblings, and oppositions to science falsely so called..."* (1 Timothy 6:20). What was Timothy to keep or guard? It was nothing less that **the gospel** itself. As people placed their valuables in hidden places for safekeeping, so God placed His inspired message in earthen vessels (human beings) and safe-guarded it by spiritual gifts from the Holy Spirit.

The noun paratheekeen (a deposit) comes from paratitheemi, a verb meaning "to entrust something to someone." The basic meaning of the term in this context means "the deposit." This noun is used by Paul again in 2 Timothy when he writes *"The good thing which was committed unto thee keep by the Holy Spirit which dwelleth in us..."* (1:14) and earlier perhaps (1:12) it may also refer to this deposit to Timothy depending on whether the subjective or objective genitive is intended by Paul. Additionally, the verb form (2nd aorist imperative, hence a command) of this word parathou is used in 2 Timothy 2:2 where Timothy is told to *"commit"* the things he heard from Paul to faithful men who will be able to teach others also.

Paul reminded Timothy that the "gift of God" in him was given to him by the laying on of hands by the Apostle Paul. The gift was not God Himself, any more than the "gift of the Holy Spirit" is the Spirit Himself! Instead it was a gift which came from God, through the laying on of hands of an apostle. This verse shows, along with 1 Cor. 9:1-2, 2 Cor. 12:12 and Acts 8:14-18, that Paul also received the baptism of the Holy Spirit, as did the other apostles, even though we have no record of the occurrence. That is why he could write that he was *"not a whit behind the very chiefest apostles"* (2 Cor. 11:5).

What spiritual gift was given Timothy (2 Tim. 1:6) we are not told. Perhaps it was the gift of prophecy, or more likely the gift of discerning of spirits. The latter fits the context of "guarding the deposit" (especially in 2 Tim. 2:14). Remember this gift of discerning of spirits was one of the nine miraculous gifts given in the first century when revelation was being given and safe-guarded (1 Cor. 12:8-10).

It is interesting to note that a miraculous gift did not dominate or take control of its possessor. Some today, who falsely claim miraculous gifts for themselves, like to contend that they are not in control when they speak in tongues (which they can't do anyway), and the Spirit just takes over their bodies. Furthermore, some contend that there were no commands given in regard to miraculous gifts, but both statements are simply not true. Paul wrote that *"the spirits of the prophets are subject to the prophets"* (1 Cor. 14:32), and the specific case of Timothy gives further evidence of the fact that he was in control of the gift, not the other way around! In 2 Tim. 1:6 Timothy was told to "stir up (better yet 'rekindle') the gift" and back in 1 Tim. 4:14 he was told to *"neglect not the gift that is in thee."*

Gems From The Greek

Prohibitions (negative commands) in the Greek language are of two types: (1) <u>mee</u> with the aorist subjunctive means "don't begin" an action, and (2) <u>mee</u> with the present imperative means "stop or quit" an action. In 1 Tim. 4:14, Timothy is urged to "quit neglecting" the spiritual gift he received, which shows that he had control of the gift, and in fact, had been neglecting his use of it! Both 2 Tim. 1:6 and 1 Tim. 4:14 illustrate that commands were given in regard to spiritual gifts in the first century, and furthermore that the possessor controlled the gift, not that a gift controlled its possessor. Hence the Spirit would not take over and mechanically force Timothy to use his gift; he must willingly consent to make use of it as its possessor.

Notice that "the gospel" was that "good deposit" committed to Timothy, and that he was to "guard" or "keep" it through the Holy Spirit which Paul said dwells "in us" – that is, in him and Timothy! In 2 Tim. 1:14, Paul is not even writing about anything "non-miraculous" when he mentions the gift given Timothy and him. Surely Paul speaks of "power," and as an inspired Apostle, he would not speak of the Spirit dwelling in him and mean a **non-miraculous indwelling,** would he? Too many today divorce the gifts of the Spirit from their first century context. We need to ask ourselves how would this be understood by those in the first century?

Gems From The Greek

Having Access

We use the term "access" in multiple settings and do so in a meaningful way. Periodically we hear someone asking, "How do I access that website?" or "Do you have access to that gated housing addition?" The basic idea behind this term is "admittance, as gaining access to an important individual," "the way or means by which a thing may be approached; as, the access is by a neck of land." It also is used to suggest liberty to approach, implying obstacles," et al.

In our New Testament, the original word prosagoogee is used three times; all usages are by the Apostle Paul. Though this specific word is not used in the LXX (Esther 4:11), it is well illustrated by the language used there. Mordecai had sent word to Esther of Haman's plan to exterminate the Jews and was requesting that she use her influence to inform her husband King Ahashuerus (Xerxes) of the plot. Esther sent word back to Mordecai that it was well-known that "*whosoever, whether man or woman, shall come unto the king into the inner court, who is not called, there is one law of his to put him to death, except such to whom the king shall hold out the golden sceptre, that he may live*," but she added, "*I have not been called to come in unto the king these thirty days.*" She accepted the challenge, saying "I will go in unto the king, which is not according to the law, and if I perish, I perish" (4:16). The King held out the scepter, a sign of permitting access to Esther to enter.

Gems From The Greek

Vine's Expository Dictionary (p. 21) says of the word prosagoogee, that literally it is "a leading or bringing into the presence of (pros, to, agoo, to lead), denotes access, with which is associated the thought of freedom to enter through the assistance or favour of another." In the remainder of this treatise, we purpose to focus upon the three usages of this word in the New Testament.

In Romans 5:2, Paul declares that due to Christ's atoning work on Calvary, Christians "*have access by faith into this grace wherein we stand...*" Surely no Bible believer doubts that a man is justified by faith. The question is whether he is justified by faith before it leads to obedience or at the point of obedience. Salvation is by grace on the part of God (Eph. 2:8-9) and hence non-earnable, yet this grace is not doled out, except through the pipeline of faith (compare Rom. 4:16 with 5:2). If we do not "stand by faith," we shall "fall from grace" (Gal. 5:4) for it is by faith that we have access to His grace (see Rom. 11:20-21).

The second time Paul employs the term "access" is in Ephesians 2:18. Here we learn that Christians "*have access by one Spirit unto the Father.*" It is interesting to note that in this verse we have all three members of the Godhead mentioned, as is also the case in 2 Corinthians 13:14. All three share in the work of redemption. How? "Through CHRIST we have access by or in one SPIRIT unto the FATHER." Earlier Jesus declared: "*No man cometh unto the Father but by me*" (John 14:6), yet the way this entrance or approach is accomplished is to believe in the Son of God, and the Bible was written for that specific purpose (John 20:31), for faith comes by no other source than by the word of God, which the Holy Spirit revealed and inspired. This introduction into the presence of God is said to be by faith (Rom. 5:2), and so it will ever be.

Whenever we contemplate the power of prayer, we automatically take into consideration that which Christ has accomplished for us in giving us access unto the Father (Eph. 3:12). We would not dare barge into a room where the president or king, or governor, was present, nor would we here in the religious realm. In the Old Testament, kings were approached through channels, and so it is with a Christian's approaching God. Christ is that channel (John 14:6), yet because of what He did, we can make that approach with boldness! Yet it must be a reverential boldness, not the smart, sassy attitude as manifested by one who begins his prayer with a chummy "Hi, Daddy!" Macknight (<u>Macknight on the Epistles</u>, p. 328) says "both Jews and Gentiles" have access to the Father by the merits of Christ's death, and concludes that thought with the remark: "Perhaps this is an allusion to the manners of earthly courts, where none have access to the prince, unless introduced by some of his servants as friends." As Paul declared, in Christ Jesus "there is no difference" between Jew and Gentile (Rom. 3:22; 10:12) even when it comes to having access to God through prayer.

Gems From The Greek

Holiness – A Requirement?

God has always demanded that His children be holy. He commanded Moses to *"Speak unto all the congregation of the children of Israel, and say unto them, Ye shall be holy; for I the Lord your God am holy"* (Lev. 19:2). But this was not required of Israel only, but of us today as well. Peter writes: *"But like as he who called you is holy, be ye yourselves holy in all manner of living; because it is written, Ye shall be holy; for I am holy"* (1 Pet. 1:5-6). Christians are described as *"a spiritual house…holy priesthood…"* (1 Pet. 2:5) and a *"holy nation"* (v. 9).

What does it mean to be holy? Do you know anyone who is? How is it possible for a person to "be holy" in an unholy world?

The word "holy" (hagios) means "to be set apart, separate from the world and consecrated to God. The term is used 229 times in the NT, with a large number of these references referring to the Holy Spirit, but other things are also described as "holy," such as a "holy city," holy angels, prophets, covenant, scriptures, ground, kiss and etc. The Hebrews were styled as *"holy brethren"* (Heb. 3:1) and Peter referred to "holy women" in 1 Peter 3:5. If these could be holy, then why can't we?

Not only can we be holy, we must be! *"Follow peace with all men, and holiness, without which no man shall see the Lord"* (Heb. 12:14), and this is comparable with Christ's statement *"Blessed are the pure in heart, for they shall see God"* (Matt. 5:8). Before we were ever born, God had determined that His people were to be holy, since

Gems From The Greek

He "*hath chosen us in him* (Christ) *before the foundation of the world, that we should be holy and without blame before him in love*" (Eph. 1:4). But how? How is it possible to be holy? SEPARATENESS is the answer. Paul commanded: "*Be not conformed to this world, but be ye transformed, by the renewing of your mind…*" (Rom. 12:1-2). God does not require of us that which is impossible. We must rely on what Christ has done, but also upon what we must do. We are to be "*holy, and without blemish*" (Eph. 5:27), and the only way this can be accomplished is by the process of separating ourselves from the world (2 Cor. 6:17-18). Yet this "lack of separation" is so difficult. Probably the biggest difference between us and our non-Christian friends is that "we go to church services on Sunday and they do not." That is not the separateness described by the NT.

Jesus describes this SEPARATENESS in His prayer to the Father: His followers "*are not of the world*," and He prays not that His Father should take them (His disciples) out of the world, yet He sends them "into the world" (John 17:14-18). There you have it – we are to be in the world, but not of the world. We are to influence the world (Matt. 5:14-16), but not vice-versa!

The English word "sanctification" also comes from the same root word as "holy." The verb (hagiadzo) is used 29 times in the NT, once as "be holy," twice as "*hallowed*" and 26 times as "*sanctify*." In the OT, unfaithful priests were condemned because they made no distinction between the holy and the common (Ezek. 22:26; 44:23), a message needed by our religious world today. No man had the right to declare something clean on his own authority.

To be holy today, we Christians must deny ungodliness (Titus 2:12-14) and separate ourselves from the world (2 Cor. 6:17). Can our friends detect such separateness in observing our lives? As one person stated it, "If you were arrested for being a Christian, would there be enough evidence to convict you?" If our life in Christ is not noticeable, something is drastically wrong. We were to put off the old man and put on the new man (Eph. 4:22-24; Col. 3:9-10). *"If any man be in Christ, he is a new creature: the old things are passed away; behold, they are become new"* (2 Cor. 5:17). This separateness involves self-denial (Matt. 6:24), including fleshly lusts (1 Pet. 2:11), youthful lusts (2 Tim. 2:22), fornication (Eph. 5:3), not viewing wicked things (Ps. 101:3), not loving the world (1 John 2:16), etc.

"Perfecting holiness" (2 Cor. 7:1) strongly suggests that this is a process, a lifelong process. We can *"become partakers of the divine nature"* by adding to our *"faith virtue, knowledge, self-control, patience, godliness, brotherly kindness and love"* (2 Pet. 1:4). How does God work on us to bring this about? He does it *"through the word of God that worketh in you that believe"* (1 Thess. 2:13). Without *"holiness, no man shall see the Lord"* (Heb. 12:14).

Gems From The Greek

"Laud Him, All Ye People" (Rom. 15:11)

In the beautiful hymn "Praise the Lord," verse four says: "Praise the God of our salvation; Hosts on high, His power proclaim; Heav'n and earth, an all creation, **Laud** and magnify His name."

What does one do when he/she lauds the Lord? This English verb is rarely used by many people today, but its cognates "laudable and laudatory" are perhaps more often found in our vocabularies than the verb itself. The word "laud" means "to give praise or express devotion to" glorify." Our English term comes from the Latin laudaare, meaning "to praise."

We are interested in this term in the Greek, since the New Testament was written in Greek. The original word used by the Apostle Paul is epaineo, a word that is used six times, once by our Lord in Luke 16:8 (translated "commended" by the KJV), and its five other occurrences were all by Paul in the following verses: Rom. 15:11 ("laud"); 1 Corinthians 11:2 ("praise"), 11:17 ("praise"), and twice in 11:22, both of which are rendered as "praise." The noun epainos is used eleven times in the N.T., nine times by Paul, and twice by Peter, and the KJV translates this substantive as "praise" all eleven times.

The verse in our text, Rom. 15:11, is a quotation from Psalms 117:1. It is interesting that both verbs are translated as "praise" in the O.T. reference (LXX, the Septuagint O.T. in Greek), even though the first occasion it is from aineo, and the 2nd verb is epaineo (same word but with the preposition added as a prefix), yet both terms are basically synonymous.

The Apostle Paul quotes Psalms 117:1 as proof that it was God's plan from of old to include the Gentiles along with the Jews as recipients of His blessings to the world through the gospel of Christ (cf. Genesis 12:3; Jeremiah 31:31-34; Galatians 3:16, 22, 28-29). The Gentiles are pictured as praising and lauding God for His plan of redemption for all mankind. The idea of commending God for what He has done is uppermost (see also Luke 16:8 where the word is translated "commended" by the KJV).

The four remaining usages in 1 Corinthians 11 (2,17 and twice in v. 22) also illustrate the concepts of praising or commending. In verse 2, Paul says he commends the brethren in Corinth when they adhere to the teachings given by him (see also 1 Cor. 14:37; 1 Tim. 1:3; 4:6, 16 and Titus 2:1). However, when they stray from the traditions which they received from inspired men, they are not to be commended. Paul bluntly rebukes them for the discord they were causing due to their attitudes toward their brethren and ultimately toward God as well. Paul states that he could not commend (or praise) them for what they were doing when they came together; what they were practicing was doing more harm than good, and he declares: "*Now in this that I declare unto you I praise you not, that ye come together not for the better, but for the worse*" (v. 17). Their actions promoted division instead of unity, and their attitude seemed to be "We want it this way, and that is the way it is going to be." Such was selfishness, instead of edifying one another. Whenever anyone today seeks to introduce innovations that are not sanctioned by the New Testament, they are deserving of the same rebuke. Periodically we have those who desire to introduce things into the worship under the guise of its being praise, or lauding the Lord, but things that are nevertheless not sanctioned by the Lord (see Col. 3:17). The word "laud" cannot be stretched to include counting beads, dancing or clapping hands in the worship. These are not to be "lauded" even though a few desire to stretch the word "laud" to include such things.

"*...despise ye the church of God, and shame them that have not? What shall I say to you?" shall I praise you in this? I praise you not*" (1 Cor. 11:22). Paul is saying that he could not commend, sanction, or approve of their actions. Their conduct was denigrating the purpose of their "love feasts," and instead of showing love for one another, it did the very opposite. Thus, they were not coming together to eat the Lord's Supper (which shows unity among brethren) because their eating a common meal together near the same time exhibited the opposite spirit - selfishness and little concern for others!

They were to be praised (commended) when they followed what they had been taught by inspired men, but rebuked when they did not, because this caused more harm than good. Such a warning is always timely, whether in the 1st century or the 21st century.

Gems From The Greek

Love and Shepherding

Following His resurrection from the dead, Jesus Christ made a number of appearances which serve as evidence that His being raised from the dead was no hoax. One of these appearances recorded by John gives us some fascinating details about Bible study and the role of the Greek language in describing the more intricate details in the life of Christ.

After dining with his disciples, Jesus asked Simon Peter, "Simon…lovest thou me more than these?" We want to call your attention to the word play that is going on in this dialogue (John 21:15-17). Three times our Lord quizzes Peter about this matter, but the actual Greek wording is often glossed over by our English translations.

Each time our Lord urges Peter that if he loves Him (Christ), he was to "feed" His sheep. Yet our Lord uses boske "feed" the 1st and 3rd time (vss. 15 and 17), but poimaine "shepherd" or "tend" the 2nd time (v. 16). It may be true that these two verbs are used synonymously, since elsewhere in the N.T. that is the case. However, the infinitive boskein is the more narrow term, and refers primarily to the feeding process, while the infinitive poimainein has reference to "herding, tending, protecting and caring for" the sheep. If John intended for a distinction to be made between these two verbs, these are the ideas inherent in the two verbs for us to consider. The fact that different words are used in the same context would lead us to assume that these are more than mere synonyms.

Gems From The Greek

Perhaps more significant is the play on words between <u>agapao</u> and <u>phileo.</u> Hugo McCord translates the section as follows: "Simon, son of Jonah, do you love me more than these?" He replied to him, "Yes, Lord, you know that I like you." Jesus said, "Feed my lambs." A second time he asked, "Simon, son of Jonah, do you love me?" Peter repeated to him, "Yes, Lord, you know that I like you." Jesus said to him, "Shepherd my sheep." A third time Jesus asked him Jesus asked him, "Simon, son of Jonah, do you like me?" Peter was grieved because a third time Jesus had asked, "Do you like me?" and replied, "Lord, you know all things. You know that I like you." Jesus answered, "Feed my sheep."

Although some maintain that these two verbs are merely synonyms, Robertson (<u>Word Pictures</u>, Vol. 5, p. 321) writes that Peter had boasted "that he would stand by Christ though all men forsook him (Mark 14:29). We do not know what passed between Jesus and Peter when Jesus first appeared to him (Luke 24:34). But here (in John 21 - wp) Christ probes the innermost recesses of Peter's heart to secure the humility necessary for service. Peter…does not even use Christ's word for <u>agapao</u> for high and devoted love, but the humbler word <u>phileo</u> for love as a friend…this time (the 3rd – wp) Jesus picks up the word <u>phileo</u> used by Peter and challenges that. These two words are often interchanged in the N.T., but here the distinction is to be preserved. Peter was cut to the heart because Jesus challenges this very verb, and no doubt the third question vividly reminds him of the three denials in the early morning by the fire…"

Gems From The Greek

It has often been expressed that Peter was hurt because the Lord asked him the same question three different times. While that may be part of the grief he experienced on that occasion, it seems more likely that on this third question, Jesus dropped down to use the same word <u>phileo</u> that Peter used consistently, and this was what it was that cut Peter so deeply. In other words, Jesus was asking him, "Peter, do you even love me the way you say you do – "liking me as a friend even though being non-committal on being devoted to me on the higher level I was discussing."

A third interesting word pair is the "lambs – sheep" usage. The first is "lambs" used by Jesus in verse 15. However, in the second and third questions posed by our Lord, He used the word "sheep." If a distinction is made between these, perhaps it would be that in the first our Lord is emphasizing younger disciples when using "lambs," while in the latter two instances "sheep" emphasizes older disciples, hence all classes of believers are included.

Finally, it is interesting that Peter himself writes that elders are to "tend (shepherd) the flock…" (1 Peter 5:2) using the more comprehensive term <u>poimaino</u>, hence not only feed, but also to protect, guard, and watch over the flock. One can't help but wonder if Peter, when using this term at the end of his life, had a flashback to the time when Jesus ask him such probing questions, including this word "shepherd" my sheep in John 21:16.

Gems From The Greek

Laying on of Hands

The action involved in the above title is used numerous times in the New Testament, but the purpose of such an action makes for an interesting study. This phrase is used to refer to the exercising of power over another, or to arrest, seize and control. At times, this phrase is used to refer to the apostles of our Lord and their imparting spiritual gifts to Christians in the first century. A third usage is the appointing or ordaining of one to an office. Now, let's take a brief look at some examples of these three types of "*laying on of hands*" in the New Testament.

At times, the Lord laid hands on individuals to heal them of various diseases, illnesses, or maladies (Luke 4:40; 13:13). Ananias laid hands on Saul of Tarsus (Acts 9:17-18) and the latter received his sight. Gifted Christians were going to be exercising this gift of healing as well (Mark 16:18). Certainly, we might expect that such powers were given to the apostles for confirming the word of God (Heb. 2:3-4) and they were so given (Acts 5:12). The verb used with "hands" varies from time to time, with tithemi (place or put) sometimes being used, as well as ballo (to cast or throw). At times the King James uses the phrase "lay hands on" someone when the actual word "hand" is not used in the original Greek. In such instances the phrase is used to translate verbs such as *krateo* (grab hold) or *piazo* (to seize).

To Impart Spiritual Gifts

Part of the "power package" received by the apostles when they were baptized in the Holy Spirit was the

Gems From The Greek

power to lay hands on Christians and give them various spiritual gifts. In Acts 8:17 the apostles *"laid their hands on them"* (the Christians at Samaria) *"they received the Holy Ghost."* Nine such gifts are listed by Paul in 1 Corinthians 9:8-10. Note that in Acts 8, though Philip himself was working miracles (v. 6, 13), yet evidently, he had no authority to impart such gifts to others. Hence, two apostles came to Samaria in order to accomplish the task. Only apostles had such authority. When we compare 1 Cor. 9:1-2 with 2 Cor. 12:12, we learn that not only was Paul an apostle, but also that the Corinthians were the "seal" of his apostleship. In 2 Cor. 12, Paul declares that *"the signs of an apostle"* were performed among these Corinthians. This must refer to something other than merely the ability to work miracles, since these Corinthians themselves could do that, and they were not apostles! What was this "sign" of an apostle? Evidently it was the laying on of hands to impart spiritual gifts. These miracle-working Corinthians (chap. 12) were proof that Paul was an apostle. When did they receive the ability to work miracles? To answer the question is to understand how they were proof of Paul's being an apostle. Later in Acts 19:6, Paul *"laid hands upon"* about twelve men and they *"spoke with tongues, and prophesied."* Now they too could be offered as proof that Paul was an apostle. Additionally, in 2 Timothy 1:6, Paul put his hands-on Timothy, thereby imparting a "gift of God" to this young man.

It should be noticed that Simon the Sorcerer knew that *"it was through the laying on of of the apostles' hands the Holy Ghost was given"* (Acts 8:18), and that he asked for this same power of "laying on of hands" (v. 19).

Gems From The Greek

To Apprehend Someone

In Acts 4:3 the inspired Luke writes that Jewish leaders "*laid hands on them*" (Peter and John) meaning "to apprehend." In Acts 5:18, the phrase is again used to signify putting someone under arrest. Both of these references use the verb <u>epiballo</u> with the noun (hands). As mentioned earlier, <u>krateo</u> and <u>piazo</u> are both used (minus the word "hands") to signify being taken into custody and translated as "laying hands upon" someone.

To Appoint Someone

In Acts 13:3, we find a third usage of the phrase "lay hands on" people being used. Here Barnabas and Saul (Paul) had hands laid upon them when they were sent out on a missionary journey. Here it means simply to appoint or ordain. When the seven men were chosen to serve tables in Acts 6:6, the laying on of hands was used in the appointment. In both of these instances, the phrase "laying on of hands" comes from <u>epitithemi</u> + the Greek word for "hands." In 1 Timothy 4:14 the elders laid their hands-on Timothy to appoint him to the task of preaching the gospel, and at the same time a spiritual gift (perhaps prophecy) was given Timothy "through" (<u>dia</u>) the imposition of Paul's hands (2 Tim. 1:6). Probably 1 Tim. 5:22 also is an example of this third type, referring to the appointment of elders.

Gems From The Greek

No Elders After 1st Century?

The battleground is Ephesians 4:7-13. The issue is the tenure of elders, and how long they were to exist. The idea that elders would to cease exist when the complete New Testament came into existence in the first century has its proponents, and that teaching has begun to spread. It is asked: "Did God intend for elders to exist after miracles ceased?"

The apostle Paul writes to our Ephesian brethren of the first century that Jesus gave gifts to men (vss. 7-8), and in verse 11 he lists apostles, prophets, evangelists, pastors, and teachers. To support the view that God did NOT intend for elders to exist after miracles ceased, one contends that the context of Eph. 4:7-13 is "miraculous gifts." It is then stated that there are four positions (offices) listed by Paul, not five, since teachers is not a separate position but is describing the office of elders previously listed, i.e. teaching elders. It is argued that all these positions are dependent upon working miracles.

Possibly expecting objections, it is argued that the position of evangelists in the church was based on miraculous gifts as were apostles and prophets. It appears that they argue that only two individuals in the New Testament are referred to as evangelists (Philip and Timothy) and both of them had miraculous gifts, which is offered as evidence they too would cease.

Not only that but they contend that the context demands that elders occupied a position in the church that also REQUIRED miraculous gifts! It is proposed that all of these positions were given to men in the church for edifying the church UNTIL the unity of the faith came, which (in their view) was the complete written revelation of God (see 1 Cor. 13).

The argument continues: We have no record of individual congregations being involved in appointing their own elders. Paul wrote to Timothy and Titus to appoint elders at the congregations where they had been left. Why did Paul not write to the congregations and tell them to appoint their own elders? one asks. There is no record of any instruction to a congregation to appoint its own elders, but only to individual men who had miraculous gifts and worked directly with an apostle. It is then stated: "This is an obvious difference between the appointment of elders and the appointment of the seven in Acts 6. In Acts 6, the church chose their own men to serve." The question is then asked, "where is a congregation's authority to appoint/install its own elders?"

Now it is time to answer the arguments given above. The fundamental error made by the proponents of the "no elders today" doctrine is that Eph. 4:7-13 is all about miraculous gifts. Due to this basic mistake, they then erroneously assert that the position of elders ended when miraculous gifts ceased. The fact is this entire section is NOT dealing with the miraculous. Such an assertion has to be imported into the context, but that means it is based on "eisegesis" not "exegesis." An examination of the context shows that Paul is discussing the "equipping" of the saints (v. 12), growing Christians unto "mature" people in Christ (v. 13), so they (and we) will not be unstable, tossed to and fro by every doctrine floating by (v. 14). We are to grow up (v. 15). **The gifts** of Eph. 4:11 **are the persons named**. This is not referring to miraculous gifts given to these men, but instead the "gifts" were the persons themselves which are named Eph. 4:11. Christ gave apostles, prophets, evangelists, elders, and teachers, etc. to mature and grow the church. Some were miraculously endowed (the first two), others were not, but all were involved in edifying the body of Christ.

The elders were also gifts given by the Lord to mature the early church. Some of them had miraculous gifts (James 5:14, 1 Peter 5:1) given them either by the baptism of the Holy Spirit (i.e. the apostles,) or by the laying on of the hands of the apostles.

The first two offices (apostles and prophets) were temporary and would not be needed when the church does its job of carrying out the task of maturing the immature saints, causing them to see the importance of *"understanding what the will of the Lord is"* (Eph. 5:17). The temporary nature of the office of the apostles and prophets was due to unique circumstances in furnishing evidence of the original proclamation of the gospel as indeed coming from heaven. The apostles had to be witnesses of the resurrection of Christ and were personally commissioned by Christ (Acts 1:22), and since the apostles had no successors, the temporary nature of their office is evident, limited to the 1st century. Their laying on their hands to impart the gift of prophecy also term-limited the office of the prophets. The fact that the first two offices listed are different from the other offices is addressed by

Gems From The Greek

Paul earlier in this same letter. The church included all Christians, but Paul specifically points out that Jesus Christ "*is the chief corner stone*" in this building, a structure (or church) which initially was "*built upon the foundation of the apostles and prophets*" (Eph. 2:20). **The apostles and prophets were foundational**, as opposed to others who composed this spiritual building (or house - 1 Timothy 3:15) called the church!

The prophets, as inspired spokesmen, were also miraculously endowed, but neither office ceased due to the cessation of miracles, nor due to what is said in this passage from Eph. 4, but rather due to the temporary nature of their office as seen in the previous paragraph. There is no exegetical evidence in the text of Ephesians 4 to indicate that the "gifts" referred to there (especially v. 8) are miraculous gifts.

Not all gifts are miraculous, as is seen regarding Romans 12:3-8, and the claim that Romans 12 is not parallel is dependent upon the false claim that Eph. 4 is only miraculous! The word for gifts in Eph. 4:8 is doma (nominative case), used four times in the Greek New Testament, and refers to anything given, as is Matthew 7:11, Philippians 4:17, etc. The word often used for gifts by Paul is charisma, a word which also signifies both miraculous and non-miraculous gifts. The fact he uses doma in v. 8 is probably because of the quotation from Psalms 68:18 [chapter 67:18 in the Septuagint (or LXX), the Greek Old Testament]. To determine if charisma and dorean is miraculous or non-miraculous must be determined from the context.

Furthermore, there is no indication that the position of evangelists was dependent upon miraculous gifts; no miraculous gifts are necessary to tell the good news, which is the meaning of an evangelist. Was Titus ever referred to as an evangelist? Did he not have a role in ordaining elders in Crete (Titus 1:5)?

The "unity of the faith" is not the complete written revelation of God. This goal of unity is not yet realized, but we are still working on it. Paul, Barnabas, Timothy, and Titus were all commissioned as church planters and evangelists, not as persons possessing miraculous gifts. Where is the scriptural evidence that miraculous gifts were the basis of appointing elders?

We now turn to answering the question: "Where is a congregation's authority to appoint/install its own elders?" Answer: It is inherent in the qualifications being given for such a work (1 Tim. 3, Titus 1:5ff., 1 Pet. 5:1-3). Who was responsible for making use of the qualification for elders? Someone is to use them for the selection of elders, or bishops! Titus was left in Crete to be in charge of this process, making sure it was done (Titus 1:5).

Incidentally, it seems strange for elders and deacons to be appointed about A.D. 65, who would only serve until the end of spiritual gifts (about A.D. 70)! "...*If a man desire the office of a bishop, he desireth a good work*" but Timothy would need to inform such a man that he would only serve for about 5 years IF this theory of no elders existed after miracles ceased were correct! "It would be hard to account for the letters of 1 Timothy and Titus in the

Gems From The Greek

canon if elders/bishops were not to be continuing ministries in the church" (Everett Ferguson).

Years ago, a movement was started which claimed that the ONLY authority elders had was through their EXAMPLE, and that only! That theory was followed a few years later by a doctrine claiming that evangelists were over the elders, since Titus appointed them (Titus 1:5), thus the elders could not tell preachers what to do!

If one looks deeply enough into the background of similar problems across the brotherhood, he may find this same basic problem. When promoters of change are stymied in promoting their ideas, they resent it, and try to remove anyone that stands in their way, even elders. If we check recent history of those advocating the removal of elders, we may see that this is just another effort to have one less group to challenge their authority.

Gems From The Greek

"No, Not to Eat"

The Apostle Paul wrote the following command to the Corinthian Christians: *"But now I have written unto you not to keep company, if any man that is called a brother be a fornicator, or covetous, or an idolater, or a railer, or a drunkard, or an extortioner; with such an one **no not to eat**"* (1 Corinthians 5:11).

Certain questions have been asked: "How absolute is this restriction not to eat?" "Are there any circumstances where a Christian may eat with a sinful brother in Christ?"

Paul had just stated by inspiration (see 1 Cor. 14:37) that a brother guilty of fornication was to be disciplined (5:1). This was to include such an immoral brother being removed from the congregation (v. 2). To the sin of fornication, Paul then adds other vices [such as covetousness (greed), idolatry, reviling (slander), drunkenness and extortion] of which Christians must not be guilty.

He then commands that they are not even to share a common meal with such sinners. How often have you been aware of such folks being disciplined, especially the sin of greed? The truth is that it is often quite difficult to distinguish between one's being a workaholic, and his being a covetous person, isn't it? Furthermore, it seems that these six sins merely represent many more which are not listed.

The point is that the Lord's followers are to be different from the world, different enough so that their everyday lives manifest that they are Christians. The world will always be filled with sinners, and Christians, instead of withdrawing from society, are to be "*lights unto the world*" (Matt. 5:14). They are sent "*into the world*" (John 17:18), yet they are not to be "of" the world. John further warns us "*Love not the world...*" (1 John 2:15-17). Problem? These Corinthians were, by condoning fornication to go undisciplined, permitting the world to come into the church, and bringing reproach upon the church. The very concept of "saint" and "sanctified" are the very opposite of that which they were condoning, even though Paul had addressed them as "saints" earlier (1:2). They were to separate themselves from such sins, and we might add "and such like" (see also Gal. 5:21).

Paul states that Christians are not to mingle with (associate with, keep company with, or be mixed up with) such unfaithful Christians. Notice that Paul (1 Cor. 10:27) and even Christ (Luke 15:1) did not object to eating and drinking with non-Christians. Why treat non-Christians differently than an unfaithful brother in Christ? It appears that in the latter case, Christians might be viewed as endorsing sinful conduct. Since Christians live in a world with non-Christian sinners does not mean they approve of the sinful things the world does, but by condoning sin in the church, it DOES APPEAR that they approve such lifestyles!

What Paul writes is not limited to the sin of fornication. Christians are not to get mixed up with such brethren lest they seem to endorse their sinful life and bring reproach on the church.

Gems From The Greek

Can we associate with them in other ways, such as social activities, invite them to sit with us at the school's ballgames, and have them over to play dominoes, just as long as we don't eat with them? It would appear that this is illustrative of any relationship which would appear to condone unrighteous conduct on the part of a sinful brother. What about inviting that sinful brother to go out with you for a meal so you can visit with him regarding his sinful life? How can a faithful Christian reprove, rebuke, and exhort (1 Tim. 4:2; 3:16) with all longsuffering and doctrine, and never have any contact with such a brother? Hence, it needs to be remembered that TOTAL non-communication is not the right procedure for us to follow, for then how is it possible for us to "*admonish him as a brother*" (2 Thess. 3:15).

Obviously, if a husband or wife be the individual who is guilty of such a lifestyle, the innocent companion is to still live with that companion. But otherwise, as one has written: "...a conscientious Christian should choose, as far as he can, the company, intercourse (communication), and familiarity of good men, and such as fear God; and avoid, as far as his necessary affairs will permit, the conversation (association) and fellowship of such as St. Paul here describes" (Macknight on the Epistles, p. 157). We dare not get mixed up and mingle with such sinful brethren so that it appears we are approving of their sinful conduct. There should be no social contact that would imply our approval of a brother's sinful conduct is permitted, but that must be tempered by the teaching of 2 Thess. 3:15.

Gems From The Greek

"Rest with Us"

In 2 Thessalonians 1:6-7, the apostle Paul says that *"...it is a righteous thing with God to recompense tribulation to them that trouble you; and to you who are troubled rest with us, when the Lord Jesus shall be revealed from heaven with his mighty angels."*

For many years, this writer has quoted this verse with the understanding that "rest" was a verb, and thus Paul was telling the Thessalonians to "rest" from their afflictions. Recently, during mid-week Bible study, the question arose in this writer's mind: "why was the word 'rest' a noun, and more specifically, a direct object type of a noun?" If Paul was not commanding these first century brethren to "rest," then what was he saying?

The subject of this clause is found in the previous verse six: GOD. Paul declares that God will repay affliction back to those who were afflicting the Thessalonians (v. 6), and not only that but He would also grant relief (rest, or relaxation) to the afflicted Thessalonians, including Paul, Silas, and Timothy, and perhaps others.

This writer also could not help but notice a close affinity between the Greek term for "rest" (<u>anecin</u>) and the modern headache medicine Anacin. Did they purposefully use this Greek word [the two terms - in English and in Greek sound just alike!] to label their headache product which brings "relief"? If so, then "How do you spell relief?" is not only by using Rolaids, but also by using Anacin.

Returning to the main point under consideration, Paul was NOT telling them: "To those of you who are troubled, rest with us," but rather was saying that God would bring relief to the afflicted. Remember that Paul warned Timothy that "*all who will live godly in Christ Jesus shall suffer persecution*" (2 Tim.3:12), and "*if we suffer, we shall also reign with him...*" (2 Tim. 2:12). With this rendering, the word *anecin* has its normal function as a direct object (or accusative case in Greek grammar).

Hugo McCord did an excellent job on these verses in his New Testament Translation. He translated it as follows: "*Indeed it is right for God to repay trouble to those troubling you, and provide relief to you along with us, who are troubled.*" I.e., **the subject "God" has a double predicate**! When would this relief come? "*...when the Lord is revealed from heaven with the angels of his power in flaming fire. He will punish those who do not know God, and who do not obey the gospel of our Lord Jesus*" (2 Thess. 2:7-8).

Other newer versions of the Bible also bear out this distinction; i.e. "rest" is not a verb, but a direct object! (Check out the New American Standard Bible; The Jerusalem Bible; The New Century Bible; Modern Literal Version; Phillips' Modern English; New English Bible.) In this instance, even the NIV (New International Version) does a good job: " [6] *God is just; He will pay back trouble to those who trouble you,* [7] *and give relief to you who are troubled, and to us as well*".

Beginning with 2 Thess. 1:6, Paul is about to discuss the truth that persecutors will be repaid for the

Gems From The Greek

trouble they have caused others. He says this is only right and just, in spite of the warped ideas of some that it would be unjust of God to recompense tribulation (hell, etc.) to wicked folks. "*Beloved, avenge not yourselves, but rather give place unto wrath: for it is written, Vengeance is mine; I will repay, saith the Lord*" (Rom. 12:19). That sounds like God is in the vengeance business, doesn't it?

God's righteousness (justice) demands that the guilty be punished, for to treat the persecutor as if he were moral and upright would not be righteousness. Next, Paul addressed "the persecuted." Who would know better than Paul (by personal experience, no less) what it is like to be a persecutor, then to be persecuted. Truly in his case, the persecutor became the persecuted! God will give "rest" (noun) to these persecuted ones at the 2nd coming.

He comes "from heaven" to render righteous judgment. For all atheists and disobedient, there's a sad day coming!" But Paul tells the Christians to whom he writes that a day of retribution is coming upon all those who are disobedient. But surely, ungodly church members, would also be included. The Universalists are wrong! It is a false theory that says that ultimately God's grace will permit universal salvation for all humanity, even though they rebelled against God and despised His grace all during their lives on earth!

And what is the nature of their punishment? Not annihilation. They will not merely cease to exist. How long would be their punishment? Everlasting destruction is just as long as everlasting life - two rewards for two peoples! God will pay the faithful with the latter, and the wicked with the former (Matt. 25:46). Sin does pay, says Paul, and its wages are death (Romans 6:23).

Gems From The Greek

Who Did What?

This article will deal with two Biblical references, one in the N.T., and the other coming from the O.T., yet both are related to the above title. One old method of teaching a Bible class, one verse at a time, has been described a teacher reading a verse, saying "well, that verse explains itself," and then move on to read the next verse. As we probably already know, this method is quite simplistic. The Bible is to be understood (Eph. 5:17), and thus Philip's question to the eunuch was "*Do you understand what you are reading?*" The eunuch's reply was "*how can I understand except someone should guide me?*" (Acts 8:3--31).

Let us take a look at John 4:2 in the King James Bible. ("*Though Jesus himself baptized not, but his disciples"*). The way this verse is constructed in English leaves us with two possible interpretations: (1) Jesus did not baptize anyone, with the exception being that He baptized His own disciples, or (2) Jesus did not baptize, but His disciples did the baptizing for Him. So, which one is it, the first or the second interpretation?

Although we may have hated the study of grammar in Junior and Senior High School, we are introduced to the importance of it again all throughout our lives. We were correctly taught that the subject of a sentence is in the nominative case, which is the case of the noun functioning as **doing** the action of a verb, while the **direct object** is a noun which receives the action of the verb. To illustrate, have you ever corrected a child who uttered "Me want to go

Gems From The Greek

outside?" He should have said "I want to go outside." His problem? He substituted a direct object for the nominative case.

John 4:2, in the original Greek, has the noun "disciples" in the nominative case. It is not in the objective case (direct object), so what is the point? The direct object does not function as the subject of the sentence, hence the disciples were NOT the ones being baptized (direct object), but were the ones doing the baptizing, thus the correct answer to the question posed in paragraph two above would be (2), Jesus' disciples were the ones doing the baptizing. Many modern translations render this correctly. Notice the following: "Although Jesus Himself was not baptizing, but His disciples were" (NASV); "although, in fact, it was only the disciples who were baptizing, and not Jesus himself" (NEB); "though it was not Jesus himself, but his disciples, who immersed" (<u>Living Oracles</u>, Alexander Campbell), and our last illustration of this comes from The Jerusalem Bible which translates it as "though in fact it was his disciples who baptized, not Jesus himself."

This is an example of the causative active verb. In our day we often make use of the causative idea with verbs in the active voice. Wallace (Daniel Wallace, <u>Greek Grammar Beyond the Basics</u>, p. 411) writes: "The subject is not directly involved in the action (in such a usage - wp) but may be said to be the ultimate source or cause of it...The subject is not the direct agent of the act, but the source behind it." Notice that in Acts 3:22, John writes that Jesus was baptizing (imperfect tense showing continuous action in the past) but then sixteen verses later he explains that it was His disciples who did the actual baptizing. Wallace states: "...the Pharisees had misunderstood Jesus to be directly involved in the baptisms (see John 4:1), for *'Jesus was not baptizing but his disciples were'* (v. 2)" [Ibid. p. 412]. Hence John adds in John 4:2 that Jesus was not in the habit of baptizing, but let his apostles take care of that (remember Paul in 1 Cor. 1:14-17?). A good translation of this verse would be: "Although Jesus Himself was not immersing them, but His disciples were."

Now let us take a look at the O.T. as we further consider the question: "Who did what?" in Genesis 14:20, we read: "*And he gave him tithes of all.*" Did Melchizedek give tithes to Abraham, or vice versa? In Hebrews 7:2, 4 we are given the inspired answer to that question: It was Abraham who gave tithes to Melchizedek. "*For this Melchizedek, king of Salem, priest of the most high God, who met Abraham returning from the slaughter of the kings, and blessed him; to whom also Abraham gave a tenth part of all;* ..." vss. 1-2, and then in verse 4 we read "*Now consider how great this man was, unto whom even the patriarch Abraham gave the tenth of the spoils.*"

Sometimes knowing the Greek language assists us in our study, but that is not always the case with every problem passage, thus we see the need of hermeneutics. Sometimes a deeper study of the Scriptures assists us, as in the case of Gen. 14:20, where we let the Scriptures themselves help us in interpreting the Bible.

Gems From The Greek

"Go To Now"

It is the latter part of the year, and since you are following a schedule of reading the Bible through within a year's time, you happen to be in the book of James. You read that James urges people to action by using the above statement in our title: "Go to now." In the original Greek, that expression literally means: "Come now," but it has a figurative meaning. Instead of meaning "come" or movement toward a person, it is a particle of exhortation, and used to gain a person's attention. This phrase is used twice in the New Testament, and only by James (James 4:13; 5:1), though it is found in extra-Biblical literature from Homer's day on down in time.

It is translated from the verb <u>ago</u>, (pronounced "ah - go,") and is conjugated as being in the 2nd person singular, present imperative form, thus a command. Both times that James uses this phrase, he adds to it an adverb of time "<u>nun,</u>" meaning now.

The term "go to now" is given various translations in modern versions, as they move further away from the literal "go" to a more figurative rendering. Notice how the following versions give a variety of ideas regarding how this expression can to be translated:

English Standard: "Come now..."

King James: "Go to now..."

American Standard: "Come now...

McCord: "Come now..."

Gems From The Greek

New International: "Now listen..."

New Living Translation: "Look here..."

God's Word Translation: "Pay attention..."

Living Bible: "Look here..."

20th Century N.T.: "Listen to me..."

New English Bible: "Next a word to you..."

Guy N. Woods (deceased) states that the purpose of this phrase "is to gain attention, and simply means (though not literally), 'See!' 'Behold!' 'Listen!' The Greek word is often used in connection with the imperative for the purpose of gaining a hearing...the implication of it is that there is something seriously wrong and those thus addressed should give careful heed to what the writer is about to set forth" (James, Guy N. Woods, p. 245ff.). Referring to chapter 5:1, Woods explains that the "come now" is 2nd person singular, but is followed by hoi plousioi, "the rich" which is plural. This is an exclamatory interjection. Those thus addressed are first singled out individually, then addressed collectively as a class" (Ibid., 256).

As suggested above, this two-word phrase "come now" is used as an interjection and has nothing to do with the literal concept of travelling. It is used to gain attention, and especially to give heed to that which the speaker is about to say! We use similar figurative expressions today in the same way, such as "Listen up," "See here," or "I'll have you to know...". V.E. Howard, in most of his radio sermons years ago, made famous the interjection "Are you listening?" James is doing the same thing in the first century by his use of this attention-grabbing phrase "age nun," meaning "listen to me now."

Woods states that weeping and howling of the rich (James 5:1) denotes "the reaction which ought to characterize those whose doom is certain. Instead of the continual round of banqueting and revelry then characteristic of them, they should weep and howl...the tenses are significant. They are to begin to weep and to continue to howl over the 'miseries' to befall them in judgment...This destiny was inevitable to them in their present condition...When the day of destruction dawned how ineffectual would their riches be! In less than ten years, a vengeance was visited upon Jerusalem and the Jews, scarcely paralleled in the world's history. When, at length, the besieged city fell before the conquering legions of Rome, the slaughter that followed was beyond description. Rich and poor were sought out and mercilessly killed; and all, without regard to their material financial condition, suffered. And, if, as we believe, the writer describes the destruction of the rich in judgment, an even more terrible destruction awaits. In view of such a destiny, these ought even now to begin to weep and to howl continuously over their ultimate destiny" (Ibid., p. 257, 258.).

Gems From The Greek

Faithful Children

In Titus 1:5-9, the Apostle Paul lists some qualifications which God requires of prospective elders to be ordained in Christ's church. In verse 6, he mentions "*having faithful children*" (KJV) but periodically there have been some disagreements over exactly what is meant when the inspired Paul uses such terminology.

Let us first zero in on the meaning of the word "children" before we move on to discuss the meaning of the word "faithful."

Obviously, the word "children" (tekna) is plural, but the problem is that this word may also be used generically, with the singular "child" and "children" being equivalent to each other. Early on, Sarah referred to the fact that she gave suck to children, even though she only gave birth to one child - Isaac (Gen. 21:7). This usage is further reinforced when noticing a number of New Testament references and then asking yourself: Is a parent with only one child exempt from what is being taught? For example: Children are to *obey their parents in the Lord*, but does an only child have to be obedient also (Eph. 6:1)? A few verses later, Paul instructs fathers not to provoke their children to wrath, but instead to "*bring them up in the nurture and admonition of the Lord*" (v. 4). Now let's apply the same question in this situation: Does this mean that a father who has only one child is not required to train him/her since the word children in Ephesians 6:4 is plural? Point? A man is not disqualified from serving as an elder (if he meets all the

Gems From The Greek

other qualifications given by Paul) simply because he has only one child!!

The second question, and a bit more problematic one, is regarding the meaning of the word "*faithful*" in Titus 1:6. The specific wording used by Paul was (and is) "tekna echoon pista." The word pista is an adjective (but can also be used as a noun: 1 Tim. 4:3, 12). In Titus 1:6 the adjective pista modifies the noun tekna, so what kind of children are being described by Paul? A brief look at different Bible versions illustrates the problem: Is this adjective to be understood as "trustworthy, dependable, reliable," etc., or does it mean "believing" or, in other words, being a Christian? Notice how the following versions treat pista in Titus 1:6:

KJV - "faithful"

ASV - "children that believe"

NKJV - "faithful"

NASV - "children who believe"

NIV - "whose children believe"
McCord - "believing children"

RSV - "children are believers"

NEB - "children are believers"

Phillips - "children brought up as believers"

Wuest - "children who are believers"

Living Oracles - "having believing children"

Gems From The Greek

Living - "children must love the Lord"

A person may be trustworthy and yet NOT be a Christian! Jesus Himself said that both the five- talent man and the two-talent man were faithful servants, ...*faithful over a few things*... (Matt. 25:21-23). These two were reliable, but the one talent man was not. You may employ a young teenager as a babysitter because you feel that she/he is reliable, but that does not imply that she is also a Christian, does it? You may give a housekeeper the keys to your house because you think she or he is trustworthy, but that does necessarily mean that she is a Christian.

The term "faithful" may also be used to describe things: Faithful **saying** (1 Tim. 1:15) and may be translated as a "true" (1 Tim. 3:1 - KJV) saying (see also Rev. 21:5; 22:6); dependable or reliable **diseases** (Deut. 28:59 LXX) where it is rendered "*of long continuance*"; and **wells** (Isa. 33:16 LXX) which are trustworthy and not likely to dry up.

But the adjective "faithful" is also used to describe God, Jesus Christ, and also a host of human beings such as Abraham (Gal. 3:9). Likewise, Clement (writing to the Corinthians) stated that Abraham, who was called the 'friend,' was found faithful in that he rendered obedience unto the words of God (The Apostolic Fathers, by Lightfoot). Others described as "faithful," were Tychicus (Eph. 6:21); Epaphras (Col. 1:7); Onesimus (Col. 4:9); Moses (Heb. 3:5), Silvanus, or Silas, who was called a "*faithful brother*" (1 Pet. 5:12); Antipas, whom Christ styled as "*my faithful martyr*" (Rev. 2:13).

Gems From The Greek

A majority of times the word "faithful" is used in describing a believer in Christ, i.e. a Christian. In fact, this is its primary usage in the Letters where a believer generally refers to a Christian (see Acts 16:1-2; 1 Cor. 4:2, 17; 2 Cor. 6:15; 2 Cor. 6:15 ("*what part does a believer have with an unbeliever?*"); Eph. 1:1; 1 Tim. 4:3 describes Christians as "*them that believe and know the truth*" (see also verse 12). The fact is that all Christians are stewards, and "*it is required in stewards that a man be found faithful*" (1 Cor. 4:12).

Hence, "*having children that believe*" (Titus 1:6) most likely refers to a requirement that a man's children be Christians at the time of his appointment as an elder in the Lord's church (at least those who are old enough). The age factor is also involved in the following edict that such children are not to be involved in riotous or unruly behavior. Thus, to be appointed an elder, a man ought to have one or more children who are Christians, and also satisfy the other qualifications listed in 1 Timothy 3 and Titus 1.

Gems From The Greek

Dung   (Phil. 3:8)

"*Yea doubtless, and I count all things but loss for the excellency of the knowledge of Christ Jesus my Lord: for whom I have suffered the loss of all things, and do count them but dung, that I may win Christ*" (KJV, Phil. 3:8).

The term "dung" refers to animal droppings, excrement or waste, feces, manure, or something repulsive. The Arndt/Gingrich Lexicon defines skubalon with various synonyms such as refuse, rubbish, leavings, dirt, and dung (A/G Lexicon, p. 765). Why would Paul use such a Greek term as skubalon in a spiritual context?

Paul had earlier in the same verse 8 used the term "loss" (zeemia) to describe his former life before becoming a Christian, and then in the latter part of verse 8, he substitutes our word skubalon for the word "loss."

Kittel's Theological Dictionary of the New Testament gives us a short history of the use of this word in extra-Biblical Greek (p. 445) as follows: "skubalon occurs only in later Gk., and is rare...Strabo (1 B.C. - 1 A.D.) uses it to refer to fodder or food that has gone bad, and also mentions its usage to refer to 'scraps' or 'leavings' after a meal." Of course, this source also mentions its usage as "excrement" and et al. Shortly after Paul's writings, Josephus uses this term to describe "how the inhabitants of Jerusalem, during the famine when the city was besieged by Titus, had to search sewers and dung for something to eat" (p. 446).

Gems From The Greek

It is evident that Paul is using the language of comparison. Jesus had earlier said that the kingdom of heaven is like a treasure hidden in a field, and a man goes and sells everything which he possesses in order to obtain that field (Matt. 13:44). Similarly, a merchant finding a pearl of great price, sold all that he had in order to purchase that pearl (v. 46). Since we are dealing with comparisons, let us answer the question Jesus posed: *"For what is a man profited, if he shall gain the whole world, and lose his own soul? or what shall a man give in exchange for his soul"* (Matt. 16:26).

In his commentary on The Letters of Paul to the Philippians, Pat Harrell states: "Paul's former accomplishments are now appraised...as refuse (skubala). While this is striking language to a modern reader, it would be shocking to a Judaizer. How shocking depends ultimately on how skubala is translated. It originally meant...that which was 'throw to the dogs.' It was a common term for that which was no longer fit for use and consequently was discarded, hence the RSV **refuse**. It was, however, also the term for 'excrement,' hence the rendering of 'dung' in the KJV (cf. 1 Cor. 4:13 where a different word is employed). In either case, it could hardly be said that the apostle was seeking to be polite. His achievements as a Jew, once so highly esteemed, were now totally offensive. It was, of course, his **gain** in **Chris**t that so completely negated his former attainments" (p. 120).

Since so many folks today have a nonchalant attitude toward spiritual matters, often expressed by the phrase "take it or leave it," (and they usually leave it!), their indifference and unconcern is appalling! They would probably label Paul as a religious fanatic, that is, until they have matured and begin to put things first! Right now, in their youth, they have a difficult time understanding how it is that Paul could feel so strongly about Christ and His church!

What they call fanaticism, Paul would call "*the unsearchable riches of Christ*" (Eph. 3:8). To the first century Jew, Paul (as Saul of Tarsus) would be considered a person to emulate; he had arrived! Instead, Paul exhorted others to follow him, but only as he followed Christ (1 Cor. 11:1). "Trusting in the flesh" for Paul was over: "*Though I might also have confidence in the flesh. If any other man thinketh that he hath whereof he might trust in the flesh, I more: Circumcised the eight day, of the stock of Israel, of the tribe of Benjamin, an Hebrew of the Hebrews; as touching the law, a Pharisee; Concerning zeal, persecuting the church; touching the righteousness which is in the law, blameless. But what things were gain to me, those I counted loss for Christ* (Phil. 3:4-7)."

Later he wrote: "*...this one thing I do, forgetting those things which are behind, and reaching forth unto those things which are before, I press toward the mark for the high calling of God in Christ Jesus*" (3:13). There is nothing more important in your life than Christ's church (Eph. 5:23). As one person said: "Paul said ' this one thing I do,' not these forty things I dabble in!" Don't be like the foolish rich farmer who laid up treasure for himself but forgot to include God in his life (Luke 12:16-21.) Now, do you see why Paul used the word "dung"?

Gems From The Greek

A Call to the Performance of a Task

The Greek verb kaleo is a very common word, found in most New Testament books, as well as in the Septuagint (LXX) and in secular Greek literature. The basic meaning of this verb is "call." It carries various shades of meaning, which is typical of most words, due to contextual considerations. Other important cognates are akin to this basic verb, such as parakleetos and even the well-known word for church ekkleesia, and the adjective kleetos (verbal adjective) as in Romans 1 where Paul was a "called" Apostle (v. 1), and Roman Christians were "called ones" (v. 6) of Jesus Christ, and also described as "called saints" (v. 7).

Another term having the stem kal but with the preposition pros affixed on the front of it, is our word for study at this time, i.e. proskaleomai. This term, found thirty times in your New Testament, is consistently rendered as "called." But there is an additional meaning that needs to be considered, since the preposition pros evidently has some function that would set it apart from the root verb kaleo. What might that be?

A number of passages have Jesus (or John, and others) calling people "to himself" (see Matthew 10:1; 15:10; 15:32; 20:25; Mark 3:13; 3:23; 6:7, 8:1; Luke 7:19; 18:16, and many other verses). The idea of "summoning" becomes more apparent when one reads all of the passages as a whole, and even the idea that some people are summoned to perform a task. For example, in Luke 7:19, John "called" two of his disciples, and sent them to Jesus to

Gems From The Greek

get some information he wanted; i.e., he summoned them to the performance of a task. In Acts 16:10, Luke tells us that Paul had a vision, after which they (Paul, Luke, and others in the traveling party) left for Macedonia. Luke describes it as: "...*concluding* (from the vision - wp) *that the Lord had **called** us to preach the gospel unto them.*"

It is noteworthy that The Analytical Greek Lexicon (pages 349-350) describes proskaleomai as follows: "...to call to, summon, invite, to call to oneself...to call to the performance of a thing, appoint (Acts 13:2; 16:10).

This verb is used in Acts 2:39 "*For the promise is unto you and to your children, and to all that are afar off, even as many as the Lord our God shall call.*" Note that the word for "call" here is not merely kaleo, but proskaleomai; this is significant! It is probable that this is not referring to the call of the gospel, but to a more specific, restricted calling to the performance of a task. This would fit the context, plus it matches beautifully with the LXX use of this verb in Joel 2:32 ("*the remnant whom the Lord shall call*"), where it is connected with the miraculous phenomena prophesied by Joel which would occur on the day of Pentecost and following (see Acts 2:16).

In the tract (authored by Ron Cosby and this writer) entitled The Gift of Acts 2:38, 39, the following comments are found at the conclusion of that treatise: "It is true that God calls sinner to salvation through the gospel message (2 Thessalonians 2:14), but the verb "call" used there is kaleo, while the verb used by Luke in Acts 2:39 is proskaleomai, meaning "to call to oneself." In the texts referring to God's summons to salvation, the verb used is kaleo, but this particular "call" of Acts 2:39 is more restrictive. Hence another verb was selected by the Holy Spirit to convey such an idea. The Arndt and Gingrich Lexicon (p. 722) mentions the verb proskaleomai being used to designate a "special task or office." More to the point, the Analytical Greek Lexicon (p. 350) lists one meaning of the term as "to call to the performance of a thing, to appoint." In Acts 13:2 the Holy Spirit "called" (the word is proskaleomai) or appointed Paul and Barnabas to preach to the Gentile world. In Acts 16:10, the Lord appointed Paul and Luke for the work in Macedonia. In these examples, Christians were "called to the performance of a thing" or in other words "appointed." It is obvious that they had **already obeyed the gospel**. Since this summons was not a "call" to salvation, the verb proskaleomai was used. The basic meaning of the term is to "call to oneself" is used thirty times in our New Testaments, but never to refer to the calling of a sinner to salvation – UNLESS ACTS 2:39 IS THE ONLY EXCEPTION! If all other twenty-nine occurrences are never so used, and if the call to salvation normally uses the word kaleo, is it not probable that something other than a call to salvation is under consideration in Acts 2:39?

It is our studied conclusion that Acts 2:39 could well be translated as follows: "*For the promise is unto you, and to your children, and to all that afar off, even as many as the Lord our God shall appoint*" (see also Acts 2:33; 1 Cor. 12:4-11, et al.).

You may order this tract from **Basic Bible Truths Publications** for a deeper study of this passage.

Gems From The Greek

Does the Holy Spirit Intercede for Us?

In Romans 8:26-27, the Bible says the spirit (pneuma) intercedes for us, but which spirit is referred to in this reference – man's spirit or the Holy Spirit?

Because a number of versions capitalize the "s" when the translators felt that the Holy Spirit was being referred to, many accept their judgment as authoritative. Surely, we can understand that when the word "spirit" is used, it may be referring to something beside the Holy Spirit, can we not? Romans 8:15, with its usage of the term "spirit," is proof that the context should be determinative. Though verses 14 and 16 may refer to the Holy Spirit, the human spirit is referred to in v. 15 in both of its occurrences within that verse.

Now let's take a look at verses 26 and 27 of Romans 8. Some brethren believe that this refers to the actions of the Holy Spirit, as the following quotation proves: "The indwelling Holy Spirit is their intercessor right here and now on the earth (Rom. 8:26)."

Others insist that these verses do not even refer to the subject of the Spirit's indwelling at all, but rather merely describes an action of the Holy Spirit occurring on our behalf before God's throne. We offer a third alternative for your consideration.

That the word "spirit" refers to the human spirit in these two verses is evident. The truth is, verse 23 makes is clear who is doing the groaning. Additionally, the overall context needs to be considered. Paul has been contrasting man's flesh with his spirit, starting back in Romans 7:14, and continues right on through the end of that chapter, and into this 8th chapter as well.

How could man's spirit intercede for himself, you ask? How could the 1st person and the third person be applied indiscriminately to the same being at the same time? Answer: We've never had that problem with other passages, such as "Lord Jesus, receive my spirit" (Acts 7:59) where Stephen distinguishes himself from his spirit. See also 2 Corinthians 4:16; 2 Corinthians 5:1,4 (note once again Paul uses the word "groan"), and certainly the immediate context illustrates the same distinction in Romans 7:23,25.

Why should we interpret the word "spirit" in Romans 8:26 to be the human spirit? (1) The absence of the word "Holy" or other modifiers used with the word "spirit" should alert us to the possibility that something other than the Holy Spirit may be referred to; (2) the first letter in the word "spirit" being capitalized means only that the translators felt the Holy Spirit was being referred to, but as we've noticed, this should be determined by the context, and other factors. Capitalizing the "s" when the word spirit is unmodified is interpretation, and the original language does not so interpret the word for the reader, but permits him to do his own interpreting; and (3) the context certainly argues for the plausibility that the human spirit is being referred to in Romans 8:26, since the contrast between man's flesh and spirit is a major theme in this section of Paul's letter.

Hence, we interpret the passage to read this way: Likewise the spirit (human spirit) also helpeth our (notice the distinction between "spirit" and "our"; i.e., the human spirit desires to serve God and, though at war with the flesh [Rom. 7:23], still wishes to help the flesh with its) infirmities: for we (the flesh, or body) know not what we should pray for as we ought: but the spirit (human spirit) itself maketh intercession for us (the human spirit intercedes for the flesh, or physical body) with groanings (these "unutterable groanings" are those of the "human" spirit [see verse 23] not the "Holy Spirit," for why would the Holy Spirit have trouble articulating Himself?) which cannot be uttered, and he that searcheth (this does not refer to the Holy Spirit because it is the wrong gender to do so) the hearts (Christ is the "heart-searcher" [see Rev. 2:18, 23]) knoweth what is the mind of the spirit (human spirit), because He (Christ) maketh intercession for the saints according to the will of God (not only is Christ the heart-searcher of verse 27, but He is also our intercessor with God, serving in this capacity in heaven on our behalf [Rom. 8:34].)

Hence, Christ serves as our intercessor in heaven, and the human spirit intercedes for the flesh on earth as we pray to the Father with unutterable groanings. This particular passage does not even touch on the subject of the Holy Spirit personally indwelling a child of God, but it does bring to a successful conclusion Paul's contrast of the flesh and spirit discussing how the two are to be distinguished.

Gems From The Greek

"Remission of Sins" Modifies Which Verb in Acts 2:38?

"In Acts 2:38, is it not true that the prepositional phrase "for the remission of sins" modifies only the verb repent?"

Answer: No, that is not true, though such an argument is often used to deny that baptism has anything to do with sin removal. Besides interpreting baptism as a "spiritual baptism," and the old argument that the Greek preposition has a causal use (hence might be translated as "because of"), this third argument is also gaining some in popularity among false teachers.

The argument is actually not new at all, because Ben Bogard, back in 1938, used it in his famous debate with N.B. Hardeman. Bogard put it this way: "You can't join repent and be baptized to the same predicate because they are different in number and person." False teachers contend that the prepositional phrase "unto (for) the remission of sins" modifies only one of the verbs, since "repent is a 2nd person plural verb, and be baptized is a 3rd person singular verb. That argument may sound good to the unwary, but it is incorrect.

To bolster their point, they argue that the two commands are NOT directed toward the same group of people. This writer would ask: "What second group is being addressed?' Thayer's Greek Lexicon makes this relevant remark: "ekastos (our word "each one" or "everyone") when it denotes individually, every one of many, is often added appositively to nouns and pronouns and verbs in the plural number." The truth is that the word "everyone" often functions as an appositive when used with NOUNS, PRONOUNS and VERBS IN THE PLURAL NUMBER.

But a quick glance at New Testament usage illustrates this very point. In Luke 2:3, we read "And all (PLURAL) went to be taxed, every one (SINGULAR) into his own city." John writes: "…ye (PLURAL) shall be scattered, every man (SINGULAR) to his own…" Paul also is included in this group, for he writes: "When ye (PLURAL) come together…this is not to eat the Lord's Supper, for in eating every one (SINGULAR) taketh before other his own supper…" (1 Cor. 11:20-21). Finally, the following command is found in 1 Cor. 16:1-2: "As I have given order to the churches of Galatia, so also do ye (2nd PERSON PLURAL), let everyone (3rd PERSON SINGULAR) lay by him in store…" As far as person and number are concerned, the similarity between these two verses and Acts 2:38 is striking indeed.

Can a singular word be joined to a plural? No, some declare, "It would be grammatically incorrect." The Bible teaches otherwise. If it were grammatically incorrect, Luke did not know it (Luke 2:3); Paul did not know it (1 Cor. 16:1-2), et al., and more importantly, the Holy Spirit did not know it, since He inspired all these men to write what they wrote! The fact is that the New Testament teaches that salvation "follows" baptism (Mark 16:16; Acts 22:16; 1 Pet. 3:21). Acts 2:38 is in perfect agreement with what the New Testament teaches elsewhere regarding the necessity of baptism for salvation.

Gems From The Greek

Saved Through Water?

In 1 Peter 3:20, we are told that "eight souls were saved through water." What is the meaning of "through" here in this context?"

The above Scripture comprises one of the most hotly debated sections in the New Testament. Since the huge majority of the religious denominations teach that baptism has nothing to do with a person's salvation, they typically try to explain away what the text plainly declares, i.e., that mankind is saved by baptism in water. For example, one person wrote: "Baptism does NOT save us, but shows that we have been saved…" (A Brief Catechism on Baptist Beliefs, I.J. Van Ness). Notice that the inspired apostle Peter declares that it does save, but modern man says "No, it doesn't." Obviously, both cannot be right, so this writer will take his stand on the truthfulness of the New Testament account.

The expression used by Peter in verse 20 regarding salvation is from the Greek verb diasozo = to save through. The preposition dia basically signifies the idea of location, i.e. going "through" a place, but a very common use is to couple it with noun in the genitive case (such as "water") and this construction of dia + the genitive = agency. Then to stress the idea of through, immediately following the verb (which has dia as a prefix), Peter uses dia again with the genitive case of water. Some understand the latter to mean "by means of water," and using the phrase as an intermediate agent, i.e. these eight souls were saved "by means of water." Others understand the use of dia as local, i.e., as safely passing through the water in the ark. Neither view (local use or the use expressing agency) does an injustice to what Peter is saying, and in both cases, the point remains the same. They were saved, water was involved and there is something here that Peter wants his readers to understand regarding their own salvation.

Certainly, these eight souls in Noah's day were saved "in" the ark ("wherein" literally means "into which" meaning the ark), and they were also saved "from" the waters of the flood, but that is not the point that Peter is making. He uses the expression "through water." Our task is not to discuss the prepositions "in" or "from" and then use them to deny what Peter said, but rather our task is to understand why Peter worded it as he did, and to understand what he is teaching.

Peter is saying that the family of Noah (Gen. 7:13) was brought safely "through the water." The flood was the means of destroying the old world which had become so sinful and ungodly (Genesis 6:5-6), but it also was the very means by which Noah's family was delivered (or saved) from that corrupt world of so long ago.

Guy N. Woods writes: "The salvation of Noah and those with him is thus made a type of the deliverance which the sinner receives in passing through the waters of baptism. The 'likeness' obtains in the following manner: (1) the waters of the flood bore up the ark and delivered its occupants from the destruction of the antediluvian world; (2) these waters separated those who were saved from those who drowned in them; (3) the flood destroyed the evils of the old world and enable Noah and his family to emerge into a new existence. In like fashion, (1) baptism is the final condition in a plan through obedience to which one is enabled to escape the condemnation of the lost (Mark 15:15-16). (2) Baptism designates the line of demarcation between the saved and the lost. (3) In baptism the 'old man of sin' is buried, and from its watery grave one comes forth to 'walk in newness of life' (Romans 6:4)."

The use of "type" and "antitype" is foremost in Peter's thoughts at this point. That "water" is regular H20 is seen in the fact that it is compared to the ordinary water of the flood, hence the baptism that saves is water baptism. Some allege that Holy Spirit baptism is that which saves us, not water baptism! Such an affirmation is simply not true! The baptism of the Holy Spirit was promised ONLY TO THE APOSTLES (Acts 1:2-5); it was a baptism consisting of power (Acts 1:8); and it only occurred in the first century (Mark 9:1). That Peter speaks of baptism in water for the purpose of being saved is irrefutable. Just as Noah's family was delivered from the old world of sin, so we are delivered from the "old" man of sin (Romans 6:6; 2 Corinthians 5:17).

In 1 Peter 3:21, the inspired writer declares that baptism saves, but it is not the Savior, Christ is! As stated earlier, dia + a noun in the genitive case (here "water") expresses intermediate agency, not primary agency! Christ is the Savior, but He does so by means. The "water" is the means (or instrument) through which God exerts His saving power. This perfectly comports with that which this same apostle Peter spoke on the day of Pentecost. When those in the audience asked, "What shall we do," Peter informed them that they must "repent and be baptized for the remission of their sins" (Acts 2:38).

Gems From The Greek

"Shall Be 'Burned Up' or 'Found'"?

In 2 Peter 3:10, the inspired writer declares: "…the heavens shall pass away with a great noise, and the elements shall melt with fervent heat, the earth also and the works that are therein shall be burned up." It is on the last four words of this verse that we want to focus our attention in this treatise.

There is quite an array of renderings of this version found in various Greek manuscripts and in ancient versions. Is it "burned up" (katakaio) = "burn up," "consume by fire"? Or is it "found" (heurisko) = "come upon," or "discover." Some may say perhaps it is "destroy" (aphanidzo) = "render invisible," or "disappear." Then again, maybe we should do as one copyist did and just omit the clause altogether! I.e., we are struggling here with the problem of textual variants within these ancient documents. A.T. Robertson states that "there are various other readings here. The text seems corrupt" (Word Pictures of the N.T., Vol. 6).

If one demands that the correct word is "found" (heurisko), that would not make sense with the context "passing away," "melting with fervent heat" (v. 10), and "dissolving" (v. 11). It is interesting to note that some early copyists (Sahidic Version, ca. 200 A.D. and one manuscript of the Harclean Syriac version) decided to add the word "not" to the verb "found." This then made the text read "the earth and the works in it were not found." The expression "not found" is present in Rev. 16:20 ("the mountains were not found…") but they did not have the

Gems From The Greek

right to add "not" here in 2 Pet. 3:10 – the negative "not" is absent from the text, unlike what John wrote in Rev. 16:20. Probably these translators added the word "not" in order to make the verb more compatible with the context and to do less violence to it at the same time. Metzger admits that heurisko seems to be devoid of meaning in the context (A Textual Commentary on the Greek New Testament, p. 706), so why add a variety of modifications to make a certain verb more palatable?

There is a better solution to the problem than to introduce a number of modifications to the verb heurisko – so what is that solution? Go with a verb which is better attested in the first place and needs no such modifications to make it more acceptable!

J.W. Roberts writes: "…If 'burned up' …is correct, the meaning is plain: 'Earth' has its literal meaning, and this repeats the previous declaration that the world is to be destroyed by fire. If 'discovered' or 'manifested' (the reading of the Vatican and Sinaitic MSS.) is to be preferred, the meaning is obscure … Peter makes it quite plain (in both the earlier verse and in the one following) that the earth will be destroyed" (1st and 2nd Peter and Jude, p. 91).

The great majority of manuscripts give evidence that the verb katakaio is to be preferred (See The Gteek New Testament According to the Majority Text, p. 703). Add to that the fact that katakaio ("burned up") also fits the context much better than the other verbs in paragraph 2 above. Of course, the Jehovah's Witnesses much prefer the use of the verb heurisko, since it better suits their agenda of

Gems From The Greek

a renovated earth. Their New World Translation (p. 1315) renders 2 Pet. 3:10 this way "…the elements being intensely hot will be dissolved, and earth and the works in it will be discovered." Strangely enough, their Emphatic Diaglott of the Greek New Testament (p. 791) says: "…earth and all works in her will be burned up." Evidently, at times, it is quite difficult to be consistent!

    To sum up, Peter teaches that "the day of the Lord" (v. 10) and "the day of God" (v. 12) are synonymous. Heat and the word dissolved are used in connection with both the heavens and the elements. All beautiful houses, lovely gardens, automobiles, furniture DISSOLVED! How foolish for man to make such items their primary interests! In view of the certainty of this world's doom, the Apostle Peter argues for holiness and godly living! Why? Because there will be a holocaust enveloping the earth and the atmosphere around it in flames. That includes not just human society (as the J.W.s claim), but also the destruction of this earthly globe. Christ said: "I go to prepare a place for you" (John 14:2). Did He go to someplace else on earth? This earth is not to be renovated – it is going to be destroyed!

    Notice Guy N. Woods argument (Questions and Answers – Open Forum, p. 148): "Heaven…is the final and eternal home of the righteous. (1) Jesus left this earth in order to go and prepare 'a place' for His disciples (John 14:2). He will return from 'the place' where He went, at the end of this age, to claim His faithful followers, and will take them to the place which He went when He left the earth (Acs2:32-34; Psalm 11:4; John 14:2). Therefore, the

Gems From The Greek

'place' to which He went to prepare for man is not on this earth but is in heaven. The phrase "The new heavens and new earth" thus figuratively describes the blissful abode of heaven, where our Lord now is, and from which place He will return to take His faithful disciples back with Him."

As Woods explained, man presently resides on this earth (from which he derives his food), and [also lives] in the heavens, from which he obtains the air he breathes (Ibid., p. 147), see (1) below. Remember that the word "heaven" is used in three senses in the Bible: (1) where the birds fly (Matt. 8:20), (where the stars are – Heb. 11:12), and (3) where God dwells and Jesus reigns (Psa. 11:4; Heb. 1:3). "Heaven and earth" = where man dwells presently, and hence the "new heavens and new earth" is a metaphorical description of future abode of the righteous!

No wonder the early Christians cried "Come, Lord Jesus" (1 Cor. 16:22; Rev. 22:20).

Gems From The Greek

The Use of Negatives in New Testament Greek

Before getting into the use of negatives in questions, perhaps it would be good to point out a few other points regarding the use of two negative particles, ou and mee (this latter Greek word has two letters, a mu and an eta, and it is pronounced "may").

In comparing how these particles are used with other words, it is clear that ou is the stronger of the two, while mee is the weaker, although both of the words mean "no."

The former denies the reality of an alleged fact and is very emphatic in doing so. On the other hand, mee is the negative to use when one does not wish to be too positive. As Dana/Mantey write in their Manual Grammar of the Greek New Testament {p. 265}, mee leaves the door open for further remarks or entreaty. Ou closes the door abruptly." A.T.

Robertson illustrated the difference by picturing a young man proposing to his lady friend. If she answers him, mee, it may only men that she wants to be coaxed a little longer, or that she is still in a state of uncertainty; but if she responds, ou, he may as well get his hat and leave at once" (Ibid., p. 266).

When the two words are put together in a compound word, ou mee, they form a very emphatic prohibition! This doubling phenomenon is found over ninety times in the New Testament. In the KJV, it is often rendered, "in no wise," with the idea being "certainly not." Though it is translated various ways (not, never, by any means, etc.), yet the basic meaning of this double negative is "certainly not" in all of its locations.

Now to the use of these negatives in questions: When ou is used, the expected answer is "yes" to whatever question is posed, while the use of mee implies that the expected answer is "no." This is true whether the mee is used by itself or in a compound with an interrogative use, such as meetis, meeti, etc. These comments become much more interesting when we see their usage in play, so let's take a look at some of these instances where ou or mee, used interrogatively, are found in the New Testament.

Questions Expecting a "No" Answer

When me is used with a question, the questioner expects his question to be answered with a "No." For example, Nicodemus asked Christ "One cannot enter a second time into his mother's womb and be born, can he?" (John 3:4). The woman at the well evidently expected Christ to answer her question with a "No" when she asked: "You are not greater than our father Jacob, are you?" (John 4:12). If she had known He was the Son of God, she would not have asked her the question the way she did! Later the Jews asked Jesus: "You are not greater than our father, Abraham, are you?" (John 8:12). The word mee is also used by Jesus in John 6:67, when He asked His disciples: "You all are not going away too, are you?" Many disciples had left Him, and though He already knew these "faithful few" would not leave Him (with the exception of one, Judas), still He asked the question, not for His own benefit, but to provoke self-examination on the part of those remaining disciples.

Pondering the miraculous works of Jesus, some Jews challenged their fellow Jews by asking: "A devil cannot open the eyes of the blind, can he?" (John 10:21). Regarding himself, the Apostle Paul asked: "Paul was not crucified for you, was he?" (1 Cor. 1:13). Paul uses mee seven times in 1 Cor. 12:29-30: "All are not apostles, are they? All are not prophets, are they? All are not teachers, are they? All are not workers of miracles, are they? All do not have gifts of healing, do they? All do not speak with tongues, do they? All do not interpret, do they?" No, no, no, no, no, no, and again no!

The compound meeti is used interrogatively by Judas when he asked Jesus: "It (the traitor) is not I, is it?" (Matt. 26:25). He had already bargained with the chief priests to betray the Lord, so this traitor worded his question the same way the other disciples did (see v. 22) with the intention of covering up his skullduggery. A few other uses of meeti are found used by Pilate when he asked: "I am not a Jew, am I" (John 18:35), by Peter: "A man cannot forbid water, can he…?" (Acts 10:47), and the woman at the well who asked her friends about Jesus: "This is not the Christ, is he?" (John 4:29). She was not admitting that she was an unbeliever, but rather she couched her question to provoke them to make their own inquiry into the matter.

Gems From The Greek

Questions Expecting a "Yes" Answer

Whenever the Greek uses the negative ou to precede a question, the construction implies that an expected answer of "yes" will be given the inquiry. For example, in Matthew 6:26, to get the disciples to remove anxiety from their lives, Jesus reminds them that God feeds the birds, and then He asks the thought provoking question: "You are of much greater value than they, aren't you?"

In Matthew 7:22, ou is found only once but it modifies all three of the questions which follow it. On the Judgment Day, says the Lord, many will ask: "We have prophesied, cast out devils, and done many mighty works in thy name, haven't we?" with all three questions expecting a "yes" answer. There is no indication that the claims made by those questioning the Lord are legitimate claims! They thought they could do these things, but the fact is that only those empowered to work miracles could do such works in the first century. If they had truly been His people, Christ would already have KNOWN them, yet He states that He "never knew" them (v. 23). In Matthew 13:55-56, four questions are asked, all of which expect a "yes" answer: "This is the carpenter's son, isn't it?" "His mother is called Mary, is she not?" The next question is also modified by the ou which negates the previous question about Mary: "His brothers are called James, Joses, Simon and Judas, aren't they?" Finally, the Jews asked, "All of his sisters are with us, aren't they?" In Luke we read "this is Joseph's son, isn't it?" (Luke 4:22).

That the Lord expects us to be students of God's word is evident by the use made of this construction of ou

Gems From The Greek

followed by a question. Numerous times the Lord asked *ouk anegnoote* ("Have ye not read...?"). These all expect a "yes" answer as posed by Christ:

"You have read what David did..., haven't you? (Matt. 12:3); "Have you not read in the law...?" (Matt. 12:5). "You have read that which was spoken concerning the resurrection, haven't you?" (Matt. 22:31). He used the same expression concerning the issue of divorce in Matthew 19:4 when He asked: "You have read, haven't you, that He that made them at the beginning made them male and female?" Truly, our Lord expects us to be a people that read and study the word of God.

No wonder Mary, Jesus' mother, pondered His sayings in her heart, since He had just asked her "You do know that I must be about my Father's business, don't you?" (Luke 2:49).

Paul made abundant use of *ou* preceding questions which he asked. In defense of his apostleship, Paul asked: "I am an apostle, am I not?" "I am free, am I not?" "You are my work in the Lord, aren't you?" Of all people who should not doubt whether Paul was an apostle or not, these Corinthians should be at the top of the list. They were proof of his apostleship, for it was from the laying on of Paul's hands that they had received spiritual gifts! Though all of these questions in verse 1 expect a "yes" answer, yet in verse 8, the apostle asks two questions in such a way showing that he expects a "no" answer to the first, but a "yes" answer to the second. Paul asks: "I am not saying these things as a man, am I?" and then he immediately asks, "The law says the same things also, doesn't it?" (1 Cor. 9:8).

Both constructions are also found within the same verse in Luke 6:39: "A blind man is not able to guide a blind man, is he?" (Answer expected is "No"). Jesus then asked: "They will both fall into a ditch, won't they" (Answer expected in "Yes?"). So, the very way the question is constructed illustrates whether a negative or positive answer is expected.

One final example is now given. In 1 John 4:20, the inspired writer reasons: "If one cannot love his brother whom he has seen, he cannot love God whom he has not seen, can he?" Though the expected answer may not always be so obvious by reading questions in English translations, the Greek makes it very obvious whether such questions expect a "yes" or a "no" answer.

Gems From The Greek

What Does the Term Ekkleesia Mean?

Preachers and teachers often use the Greek word 'ekkleesia' in their lessons. What does that term mean?

Whenever the New Testament church is discussed, the word ekkleesia will surely be found somewhere in that discussion. The basic meaning of the term is seen in the construction of the word itself, since it is composed of the preposition ek (signifying "out of") attached to the front of the Greek noun kleesis, "a calling" (cf. the verb kaleo, meaning "I call").

The term ekkleesia, used 115 times in your New Testament, has more than one meaning. It can refer to an assembly that is even non-religious in nature for in Acts 19:32 it refers to a mob (yet still a group perceived as "called out" from their homes). A few verses later (v. 39) it refers not to a mob, but to a lawful assembly meeting together to take care of civic affairs. In both of these references, the word is translated "assembly" (KJV).

The bulk of the other occurrences of this word are used in a religious sense. Whenever used to designate Christ's ekkleesia, the word takes on a much more important connotation. When used to speak of all of Christ's faithful followers here on earth, it is used in its universal sense. When speaking of individual, local groups of the Lord's followers, it is being used in a congregational sense as in manifest in Romans 16:16; Acts 11:22, et al. However, it is never used in a denominational sense in the New Testament.

Gems From The Greek

All the local congregations in the New Testament were a part of that one church that Christ promised to build (Matt. 16:18). Unlike modern denominationalism, all the churches in the New Testament were to teach the same thing (Gal. 1:6-9; 1 Cor. 1:10-13; Rev. 22:18-19; et al.). Paul taught the same doctrine in the churches of Galatia as he did in Corinth (1 Cor. 16:1), as he did in every church (1 Cor. 4:17). The New Testament knows nothing of an "invisible" church to which all denominations belong, whether Baptist, Methodist, Lutheran, Catholic, et al. All denominations came into existence due to a disagreement in doctrine with, and a split off from, a religious group which preceded them. The Lord established His church in the 1st century just as He wanted it to be. It was not an amalgamation of religious groups all wearing different religious names, teaching contradictory doctrines, and governed by humanly devised organizational schemes.

Our English word "church" is derived from the Greek term kuriakos, basically meaning "of the Lord." The New Analytical Greek Lexicon states: "pertaining to the Lord Jesus Christ, the Lord's, 1 Cor. 11:20; Rev. 1:10," describing "the Lord's Supper" and "the Lord's day" respectively. The word kuriakos is an adjective and comes from the word kurios, signifying lord, Lord, master, owner, etc.

The church of Christ today is the same as it was in the first century in organization, name, worship, and doctrine. Satan has done a snow-job on the masses, especially with his doctrine that following a pattern is not important. When the church changes so much that it is no longer recognized by Christ as belonging to Him, it has become a denomination (cf. Rev. 1:20 with 2:5), that is following the doctrines of men (Matt. 15:9) instead of the New Testament.

Gems From The Greek

Many Uses of the Present Tense

We have all heard of past tense, present tense, and future tense from our youth up, but would it surprise you to learn that the idea of tense is a bit more complicated than that? For example, each of these three tenses can be further divided into more categories, due to usage made of a tense. For example, your wife may say to you: "I am in the bathroom," but that is just her way of letting you know that if the phone should ring, it is your responsibility to answer it, since she plans on taking a bath!

The fact is, she is not in the bathroom at present, but is still in the living room with you when she made that remark. However, she plans on being in the bathroom in a matter of a few minutes. Should she have said, "I will be (future tense) in the bathroom" or is it acceptable for her to use the present tense, i.e. "I'm in the bathroom" as she literally walks beside you on her way to exit the living room?

Since the speaking of a language preceded the writing of grammar books about that language, we can readily see the value of the use of context in discussions with others. Special uses of the present tense come from the way that people express themselves in various contexts. For example, one Greek Grammar lists a number of different types of the present tenses, such as the progressive present, the customary present, the point action in the present, a futuristic present, historical present, et al. Such categorizations help modern students to understand the finer shades of meaning intended by the writers of a document.

Dana and Mantey, A Manual Grammar of the Greek New Testament, defines the futuristic present tense as denoting "an event which has not yet occurred, but which is regarded as so certain that in thought it may be contemplated as already coming to pass" (p. 185). Matthew records in two places (Matt. 26:2, 24) that Jesus "is delivered up" - present tense - even though it was two days before the fact! Interestingly enough, in Genesis 17:5 (LXX) God says to Abraham: "I have made thee a father of many nations" (but "have made" is perfect tense in the Septuagint), yet the New American Standard Bible translates it as: "I will make you the father of a multitude of nations." Hence, we see that both the present and perfect tenses may express futurity!

The historical present mentioned in paragraph three above, "is characteristic of Mark 5:15 (cf. 'they come and see' [instead of came and saw]), and John. John 20:1-18 supplies an excellent example of weaving together historical presents, imperfects, aorists, perfects and pluperfects with great dramatic effect. There are eighteen historical presents here, nine simple presents and one futuristic present ('I ascend,' Jn. 20:17). Luke evidently does not like this idiom, for, in following Mark's narrative, he changes all of these historical presents but one: 'one comes' (Lk. 8:49). Both Mark and John write with dramatic effect, while Luke writes with more polish and elegance of style" (An Exegetical Grammar of the Greek New Testament, W.D. Chamberlain, p. 71).

Gems From The Greek

The present tense of "go up" in John 20:17 is clearly futuristic, for obviously "I ascend to my Father" had not happened, nor was it occurring, at that time Jesus uttered those words. "The ship sails tomorrow," in our English language means "the ship will sail tomorrow." An example of that is seen in John 14:3: "If I go...I will come again..." of the KJV is present tense, as used by John. Since it is so obvious that the context is future, the KJV translators used the future tense to translate this futuristic present.

Daniel Wallace writes: "The present tense may describe an event that is wholly subsequent to the time of speaking, although as if it were present." For example, the Greek verb mello may describe that which is about to happen, or it may be emphasizing the certainty of that thing happening. In case of the latter, it may be rendered "is certainly going to, will." "Only an examination of the context will help one see whether this use of the present stresses immediacy or certainty. In this respect, the ambiguity of the semantic nuance of the completely futuristic present is akin to the ambiguity of the lexical nuance of mello (which usually means either "I am about to" [immediacy] or "I will inevitably" [certainty]).

In John 4:25, we read: "Messiah comes" and probably is emphasizing certainty. Again, in Romans 6:9 Paul wrote: "Christ dies not" and it is certainty that is being stressed, since the verb is preceded by ouketi, with the NASV translating it "never to die again."

Hence, we see that simply to say that a verb is in the present tense may leave a wrong impression, for the present tense has many varied shades of meaning.

Gems From The Greek

"The Demoting of Christ" # 2

Though claiming to be following Christ, the Christ of the Jehovah's Witness sect is not the Christ you read about in the New Testament! These folks are infamous for their mistranslation of John 1:1: "[T]he Word was a god" (New World Translation of the Holy Scriptures, 1961). Yet in their Emphatic Diaglott (Greek text alongside of their English translation of that text), we find the following English rendering, "In the Beginning was the Logos, and the Logos was with God, and the Logos was God" (Emphatic Diaglott, 1942). Which of the two works of theirs is the correct translation? It appears that the Jehovah's Witnesses find it very hard to be consistent, and when one digs deeper into the book of John, their inconsistency is even more glaring.

Note that in the first chapter of the Gospel of John, the Bible student will find the word God (Theos) a dozen (12) times. Now the Witnesses claim that in John 1:1, the 2nd usage of the word "God" does not have the article before the noun, and thus it ought to have been translated in English by an indefinite article (a, or an); i.e. in their view, one ought to translate such an anarthrous substantive indefinitely (no article before the noun).

The Witnesses have a problem even before one gets out of the first chapter. John uses Theos 5 times in chapter one without the Greek article (the word "the"). Those occurrences are verses 1c, 6, 12, 13, and 18.

- John 1:6 — The NWT (New World Translation) translates it this way, "There

Gems From The Greek

was a man that was sent forth as a representative of God: his name was John." Now because they translated John 1:1c as "a" god, why did they not do the same in verse 6? If they had been consistent, they would have translated it thusly, "There was a man that was sent forth as a representative of a god: his name was John." Did their own translation committee just hope that you would not notice the change they made in verse 6?

- John 1:12 — The NWT renders the Greek text this way, "However, as many as did receive him, to them he gave authority to become God's children…" John uses no article in front of the word Theos, yet their NWT did not follow the rule they employed in verse 1c, and translate it as "a" god. In fact, their Diaglott also gives it as "children of God," and correctly so.

- John 1:13 — The NWT translates the anarthrous Theos as, "[T]hey were born… from God." Why did they not translate this verse as being "born from a god" as they did in verse 1c? Would not consistency demand such?

- John 1:18 — The NWT translates Theos as God (capital "G"), even though it is anarthrous in this verse as well. Here is the way they give it in English, "No man has seen God at any time; the only-begotten god who is in the bosom position with the Father is the one that has explained him." The NWT does a terrible job on this verse. Why is that? Because first of all, John only wrote the word "God" once in the Greek text in this verse, not twice! They mistranslated the word "son" in Greek and decided to substitute the word "god" for the word "son." This would then fit their agenda of not referring to Christ as "Son of God" and make verse 18 agree with their mistranslation of 1c ("a god")! Furthermore, their translators of verse 18 surely realized that when the word "God" occurs in this verse, it does not have an article used with it. Hence, our question also is applicable here, "Why did they not translate the anarthrous use of God as "a god" in the beginning of this verse like they did in 1:1c?"

The other seven times that John uses the word Theos in chapter one, all have the article "the" before the word Theos. Now, let us turn our attention to the rest of the Gospel of John. Can you imagine John writing the following…

- John 3:2 — "…a teacher come from 'a' god?"

- John 3:21 —"…they that are wrought in 'a' god?"

Gems From The Greek

- John 8:54 — "…ye say that he is 'a' god of yours?"

- John 9:33 — Can you imagine the healed blind man saying, "…If this man were not from 'a' god, he could do nothing"?

- John 10:33 — At least the NWT in this verse is consistent with John 1:1c (in their perversion of the text) for they render it as follows, "Though being a man, (you) make yourself god" (small g). We do not have to surmise here; they did it again!

- John 16:30 — "…You camest forth from 'a' god?" They did so in verse 1c; why not do it here?

- John 17:3 — "…'an' only true god"?

- John 20:17 — "…'a' god of mine and 'a' god of yours"?

In all eight of the references immediately above, John uses Theos without an article, yet in only one of them (John 10:33) does the J.W.'s perversion (the NWT) translate this usage as "a god." That is because it too, as in John 1:1c refers to Jesus, and to refer to Jesus Christ as God is anathema to the J.W.s! The fact is that the Bible does refer to Christ as God. Thomas recognized that when he said to Jesus, "My Lord and my God" (John 20:28), and Thomas did use the article when he called Jesus "God." The translation committee of the NWT thus exhibits their intellectual dishonesty in their rendering of the inspired text.

"In the beginning was the Word, and the Word was with God, and the Word was God" (John 1:1). This statement, from the pen of the inspired Apostle John, gives us three propositional truths: (1) The Word (Jesus Christ - see v. 14) is eternal in nature; (2) the Word was "with" God in the beginning; and (3) the Word was just as much "God" as was the Father whom He was "with."

When a student initially embarks on the rough sea of learning the Greek language of the New Testament, he soon comes face to face with the use of the article. The basic function of the definite article (our word "the") is to identify, that is, to set apart a noun as being distinctive. Robertson states that when it is not used, the noun may or may not be definite. Other things serve to make a noun definite also, such as demonstrative pronouns, possessive pronouns, etc., but the use of the article certainly makes it definite.

One must use the definite and indefinite articles (our words "a" and "an") with discrimination in our English translations. The Greek has no indefinite article ("a" or "an"), and thus the absence of the definite article means the noun might be indefinite, and translators may render it in English with the indefinite article when the English sense demands it. Oikia may be "house" or "a house," depending upon which is better as demanded by our English grammar.

Gems From The Greek

The absence of the article in John 1:1c is the basis for the Jehovah's Witnesses translation of the noun as indefinite, hence rendered by them as "a god." Is there another grammatically correct translation, which does not place itself in direct conflict with other references in the inspired text that state bluntly that Jesus Christ was just as much God as was the Father and/or the Holy Spirit?

Note the following comments of various linguistic authorities:

(1) When identity is prominent, we find the article; and when quality or character is stressed, the construction is anarthrous (that is, without a definite article - "the") says Dana and Mantey.

(2) Tenney remarks

The Greek word Theos, translated God, is employed here (in John 1:1c) without the article. In the second clause, the article is used: "The Logos was with the God." When the article is used, the emphasis is on the individuality, God as a person; without the article the emphasis is on quality, God as a kind of being. The use of the word 'divine' would be a fair translation, were not its modern connotation considerably weaker than the intended meaning of the text. "Deity" is a better rendering. "The Word was deity" clearly asserts that the LOGOS possessed and eternally manifested the very nature of God.

(3) Wallace explains that what is known as Granville Sharp's Rule also illustrates that Theos in John 1:1c is qualitative, and that all of the attributes possessed by "the God" (1:1b) are also possessed by Jesus Christ. The

Gems From The Greek

Word was God and yet was distinct from the Father! There are 80 such constructions in the New Testament, which match the requirements of Sharp's Rule. However, just what is that rule? It is as follows: When you have two descriptive nouns, and the conjunction "and" connects those two nouns, and the first noun has the article (the word "the") but the second noun does not, then both nouns are referring to the same person. However, in such cases, neither noun is impersonal, neither is plural, and neither is a proper name. What is so important about Granville Sharp's Rule? Both Titus 2:13 and 2 Peter 1:1 affirm the deity of Jesus Christ, just like John 1:1c. Titus 2:13 states, "Our great God and Savior, Jesus Christ..." while 2 Peter 1:1 says, "...Our God and Savior, Jesus Christ." Thus, both verses state that Jesus Christ was both God and Savior. Note that neither "God," nor "Savior" are proper names (like Jesus, John, Philip, etc.). Neither is impersonal, but rather personal, and neither is plural, but rather singular.

One cannot deny that the articular construction (ho Theos) stresses identity, and that the anarthrous construction (Theos) emphasizes character! One cannot deny that the former construction in John 1:1b says that Jesus Christ was in the presence of God the Father, and that this verse differentiates between the two, thus this shows the basic tenet of the Oneness-Holiness Pentecostals to be false! That the latter construction in John 1:1c refers to the character, quality, or attribute of Jesus being God, or Deity, is evident, not only because of the points of grammar already mentioned, but also because of the fact that the Bible does not contradict itself, which would be the case if the Jehovah's Witnesses' translation were correct.

Gems From The Greek

Far from being an emanation from God, the Word (Christ) was co-eternal with the Father Himself, existing in the beginning. What is meant when it is asserted that the clause "the Word was God" refers to the character or nature of the Word (Christ)? Is it not God's nature to create, to reveal Himself, and to redeem His creation as this very context teaches? Instead of being some intermediate created being, Christ was on equality with God (Phil. 2:6), was present with God in the beginning, and was as much God, or Deity, as was the Father Himself. This is the only explanation that does justice to the grammar and to what the Bible teaches elsewhere about Christ's deity. The Jehovah's Witnesses' translation (the Word was "a god") downplays the deity of Christ and denies the fact that the Bible does declares elsewhere that Christ is God (John 20:28; Isa. 9:7; Titus 2:13; 2 Pet. 1:1; 1 John 5:20). In fact, the Hebrew writer informs us that God the Father even called His own Son by this very term, "But unto the Son he saith, 'Thy throne, O God, is forever and ever...'" (Heb. 1:8).

Although the Jehovah Witnesses' translation ("the Word was a god") may be a grammatical possibility, and to the Witnesses themselves a probability, yet it is a Biblical and doctrinal impossibility! No legitimate translation renders this clause in such a fashion, and the fact that the Witnesses had to make their own translation to fit their doctrine ought to make the finished product suspect!

"In the beginning was the Word, and the Word was with God, and the Word was God" (John 1:1). The Word was Deity, and "became" flesh (note the distinction

Gems From The Greek

between the verbs "eimi," meaning, "to be" in John 1:1, and egeneto = "to become" in John 1:14). Though the Word existed with God from times eternal, yet when He "became" flesh and He was born of the virgin Mary, He "became" something that He was not before!

The Jehovah's Witnesses' mutilation of this beautiful passage to fit the false doctrine they concocted serves as an excellent example of the following truism, "The learning of a little Greek can be a dangerous thing!"

Gems From The Greek

The Word 'For' in Acts 2:38 – 'In Order to' or 'Because of'?

What is the meaning of the word (eis) in Acts 2:38?

Years ago, a Baptist preacher friend of mine asked: "Aren't you saying that all people have to know Greek?" My response to him was short and to the point: "Not if you folks would quit trying to confuse people and simply let them read their own Bibles in English without trying to deny what the English says!"

The preposition "for" **in English** may mean many things such as "in order to," "on behalf of," "in support of," and even "because of." However, just because the English preposition has multiple usages in English does not mean that the word eis ("for") in Greek also has those same meanings! This is a cardinal mistake of many Bible students. Just because we can say that a man is in jail "for" murder, and it means "because of" in this context, that does not mean that we can substitute freely, selecting whichever meaning might fit our preconceived opinions.

The preposition eis in Greek is used 1773 times in the New Testament, and it is always prospective ("in order to") but never retrospective ("because of"). Our Baptist friends admit that the usual meaning of this preposition is "unto" or "in order to," but they continue to insist that it can also have a causal use, i.e. that instead of baptism being necessary to achieve remission of sins, it can mean that baptism is done "because sins have already been remitted." J.R. Mantey says that one can interpret it according to his theology. However, Lexicons, grammars, et al. illustrate

Gems From The Greek

that <u>eis</u> with the accusative case, especially after verbs of motion, firmly establish the idea of extension, hence meaning "into," "unto," "towards," "for," et al.

Ralph Marcus took Mantey to the woodshed when the two debated (<u>Journal of Biblical Literature</u>, June 1951). Marcus wrote: "If, therefore, Prof. Mantey is right in his interpretation of various New Testament passages on baptism and repentance and the remission of sins, he is right for reasons that are non-linguistic." Baptists counter by arguing that Luke 11:32 and Matthew 12:41 use <u>eis</u> with a causal meaning. The Ninevites repented "at (<u>eis</u>) the preaching of Jonah," but, Mantey argues, it's obvious it was "because of" his preaching, therefore <u>eis</u> can mean "because of." Even here, the preposition carries its usual meaning: the people of Nineveh reacted TOWARD the message of Jonah. **This is what the preposition is showing, i.e. movement toward the message, not an action "because of" the message!**

A.T. Robertson, in his <u>Word Pictures in the New Testament</u> (Vol. III), states: "One will decide the use here according as he believes that baptism is essential to the remission of sins or not. My view is decidedly against the idea that Peter, Paul, or any one in the New Testament taught baptism as essential to the remission of sins or the means of securing such remission. So, I understand Peter to be urging baptism on each of them who had already turned (repented) and for it to be done in the name of Jesus Christ on the basis of the forgiveness of sin which they had already obtained" (pp. 35, 36). Hence J.R. Mantey agrees with Robertson. It is strange that Robertson (and also

Gems From The Greek

Mantey) would argue that Peter and Paul would never teach that baptism was necessary to secure remission of sins, when that is the very thing Ananias commanded Saul (Paul) to do in order to have his sins washed away (Acts 22:16)! Furthermore, in <u>A Grammar of the Greek New Testament</u> (p. 389), Robertson discusses the limits of syntax, and states: "After all is done, instances remain where syntax cannot say the last word, where theological bias will inevitably determine how one interprets the Greek idiom…So, in Ac. 2:38 eis does not of itself express design (see Mt. 10:41), but it may be so used. When the grammarian has finished, the theologian steps in, and **sometimes before the grammarian is through** (emphasis mine – wp)." Dear reader, Mr. Robertson's comment regarding "bias" describes the basis of his argumentation in his <u>Word Pictures</u> on Acts 2:38!

"*…in the name of…*" In Matthew 10:41-42, Jesus uses the phrase "*in the name of*" three times (in the name of a prophet, a righteous man, and finally a disciple). All three of these usages stress the same point of an action being done for the purpose of, with a view toward, reaching a goal. Yes, one could have performed these actions because he was already that kind of person, **but that was not the point which Jesus was emphasizing**! Each verb (i.e. "receiving" [used twice in v. 41} and "giving" [used once in v. 42]) urges action "with a view toward BEING a certain type of person"; it was a goal to be achieved, not one already achieved, similar to hoping for heaven (Rom. 2:24), and/or stretching to reach a goal (Phil. 3:12-14). The Lord was informing His disciples that when He sent them on that limited commission, those who received them and

Gems From The Greek

their message, would be rewarded. Such believers would move from non-receptiveness to the sphere of being receptive. This is parallel to what the Ninevites did in Matthew 12:41. It is receiving one **into** the position (or treatment) of a prophet, a righteous person, or a disciple, and hence eis + the accusative case continues to signify movement toward a goal, as in all of its 1773 usages in the New Testament.

    J.W. Roberts, in discussing Acts 2:38, disagrees with Robertson. Roberts declares: "There can be no valid reason for not connecting both repentance and baptism with the remission of sins" (and surely Robertson would agree that bias is not a valid reason! - wp). Roberts continues: "Later teaching of the New Testament confirms this view (Acts 22:16; Rom. 6:1ff; 1 Pet. 3:21), and modern scholarship is overwhelming in supporting it. For a parallel use of "for remission of sins" see Matthew 26:28, where Jesus' blood is said to have been shed "for remission of sins." So, we see that Christ's shed blood, repentance, and baptism are all "for the remission of sins." To argue that baptism in Acts 2:38 is NOT for the removal of sin, yet repentance is, shows extreme bias. Whatever repentance is for in this verse, so is baptism! But if baptism is done because sins have already been forgiven (as per Robertson) then repentance would also be commanded because forgiveness of sins had already been obtained. Such reasoning would necessarily argue that both repentance and baptism have nothing to do with remitting sin. Obviously in Acts 2:38 Peter is not saying that repentance and baptism have different purposes (i.e. with the former being in order to obtain, while the latter is because one has already obtained) in relation to the forgiveness of sins, because both verbs stand in the same relationship to the preposition eis.

Finally, to argue that an interpretation "makes sense" does not demonstrate that such is an acceptable meaning to give to a word. To express "because of," inspired writers could have used dia + the accusative case, but they didn't do that in Acts 2:38. Here, as in all other 1772 usages in the N.T. (including those located in Matthew and Luke previously mentioned), the word eis is prospective, thus Acts 2:38 teaches that baptism is "in order to obtain" the remission of sins. If Robertson and Mantey are correct in their interpretation of various New Testament passages on the non-essentiality of baptism, repentance, and the remission of sins, they would be right for reasons that are non-linguistic, i.e. religious bias!

Gems From The Greek

Does 1 Cor. 13 Refer to the Completion of the New Testament Canon?

Question: "We've taken '*the perfect*' or 'the complete' in 1 Cor. 13:10 to mean the New Testament canon. This cannot be. First, in the Greek, the phrase CANNOT grammatically refer to the Scriptures. Second, the verse says that prophecy, tongues, AND knowledge will pass away at that time. Are we saying that knowledge is no longer a current item?"

Answer: The querist is mistaken in his above contention. By referring to the original Greek language in which the New Testament was written, he possibly had in mind the fact that we ought not compare James 1:25 ("*perfect law of liberty*") with 1 Cor. 13:10 ("*that which is perfect*"). If that is what he means, and he has stated it poorly, then he has a point. It is incorrect to use the word "law" in James 1:25 and argue that the same adjective (teleion) also refers to "law" in 1 Cor. 13. WHY? The Greek word teleion can be either masculine and neuter in gender, but since an adjective in Greek must agree with the noun it modifies in gender, number, and case, we have a problem. In James 1:25 it is masculine since it modifies a masculine noun "law," but the word teleion in 1 Cor.13:10 (though spelled the same as in James 1) is neuter, since it has the neuter article used with it. James is referring to "law," while Paul in 1 Cor. 13:10 refers to a "*perfect_____?*" WHAT? Well, it can't be Christ at His 2nd coming because the word is neuter, but the word "Christ" is masculine gender, not neuter!

Gems From The Greek

The best choice is that one usage that Paul himself wrote about when he referred to "*that perfect WILL OF GOD*" in Romans 12:2. Since the "*will*" is neuter, Romans 12:2 is a more correct example to illustrate what "the perfect" of 1 Cor. 13:10 refers to, and to cap it off, Paul was the writer of both passages.

But can the term "perfect" be used to refer to the N.T. canon? Yes, that's the understanding of the Romans 12:2 reference. The word teleion (complete or mature) is used many times in the N.T. Besides the above references, it is used to refer to **mankind** (Matt. 19:21; Phil. 3:15; Col. 1:28; James 1:4, 3:2), to **work** (James 1:4), to **love** (1 John 4:18), etc. To say this term could not apply to the New Testament canon is erroneous indeed, making a law based simply upon one's own "say so." The N.T. does the very thing that the author contends "cannot be done" and it does so under two different figures ("*law*" – James 1:25, and the "*will*" of God – Rom.12:2). Call it what you wish – the will of God, the law of liberty, the gospel, the Scriptures, the faith – the term "perfect" or "complete" can be used with them all (Jude 3), since this adjective is used with all three genders: masculine, feminine, and neuter (Arndt/Gingrich Lexicon, p. 816).

Additionally, the very context in which the reference (1 Cor. 13:10) is found makes it clear that reference is made to the N.T. canon. Paul contrasts the "partial" with the "complete." That partial message, delivered by inspiration during the earlier part of the period when revelation was being given in the 1st century, was not discarded nor done away. If it was not done away, then why then does Paul write that the partial "shall be done away"? (1 Cor. 13:10). Because it no longer would exist "in part," in bits and pieces, but would be incorporated into "the complete." It was combined with revelation given later during that period, gathered into a complete whole, and then inspiration was transferred to an inspired book that came from inspired men! And when we read it, Paul declares that we too can understand his knowledge in the mystery of Christ (Eph. 3:3-4). Paul's KNOWLEDGE was miraculous; our KNOWLEDGE comes from reading what he wrote!

In our querist's quibble regarding knowledge, he asks "Are we saying that knowledge is no longer a current item?" He sits up a "straw man" for the sole purpose of knocking it down. I know of no sound gospel preacher who does not make a distinction between "present day KNOWLEDGE" and the KNOWLEDGE spoken of in 1 Cor. 13:8. The latter is a knowledge that does not come by learning and/or life's experiences, but rather that which was a miraculous gift in the 1st century (nine such gifts are listed in 1 Cor. 12:8-10) and notice that KNOWLEDGE is specifically mentioned in v. 8. Nobody is saying that knowledge is no longer present in our world, but we are saying that the supernatural gift of knowledge has vanished away, along with speaking in tongues, and all other such miraculous gifts given in connection with God's revealing His will in the first century.

Gems From The Greek

Old Man - New Man (Rom. 6:6; Eph. 4:22-24; Col. 3:9-10)

Three times the Apostle Paul utilizes the "old man – new man" contrast (listed above) in his inspired writings in the New Testament, and in doing so he very effectively describes what it means to be converted to Christ. The adjective used in the three references above is palaios (cf. palaeology, etc.) signifying "old in years; i.e., that which is of long duration." When a writer desired to emphasize the beginning or origin of a thing as being old, he would use the Greek term archaios. Vines Expository of New Testament Words (p.135) quotes Abbott-Smith Greek Lexicon saying the "palaios denotes old 'without reference to beginning and origin contained in archaios' a distinction observed in the papyri (Moulton and Miligan Lexicon)."

Since Paul is describing that which is old and worn out, the word palaios was selected by the Holy Spirit from Paul's vocabulary. Palaios is this context describes what belongs in the past, i.e. a believer's former self before conversion, hence his "old man." No doubt Paul could have used this analogy to contrast his former life as a persecutor of Christians with his later life following his conversion (see Romans 7:14-25). When a child receives a wagon for his birthday, he is proud of it, and desires to quickly show it to his friends. After a few years, that wagon begins to show its age. Then perhaps 5 years later, his parents purchase a new red wagon for him. Question: When did the first wagon become old? Obviously when it was replaced by a new, shiny red wagon (with all four wheels intact!). The old man, says Paul, became old when he was superseded by the new man!

Let us examine each of the above three references in their own individual contexts.

Rom. 6:6

After becoming a new man, the Christian (though saved by grace) is obligated to adjust his/her behavior and begin living righteously (Rom. 6:1). Grace has never included the license to sin (v. 2). In verses 3-4, Paul states unequivocally that baptism is a line of demarcation between the old and new man. When one is baptized into His death, he contacts the blood of Christ which was shed for the remission of sins (Matt. 26:28; Rom. 6:3). It is at this precise point that the newness of life occurs, the old man is crucified (v. 6), and our life as a new person in Christ begins.

This is why the old life of sin must cease (v. 12). Paul is saying that the man cannot "blame the devil" since the new man is responsible for who or what controls his life. We are not to let sin "rule" neither *"yield our members as instruments of unrighteousness."* The point is that we are to be in control, and we are required to make the right decisions regarding own behavior.

We as individuals decide who it is that we are going to serve. We are either slaves to sin, or slaves of obedience unto righteousness (v. 16).

"*But God be thanked, that ye were the servants of sin, but ye have obeyed that form of doctrine which was delivered you. Being then made free from sin, ye became the servants of righteousness*" (Rom. 6:17-18).

Paul is not saying that he was glad that the Roman Christians were once sinners, but rather that they changed from being that old man, and became a new man, serving God. When did that happen? When they "*obeyed that form of doctrine*" (v. 16). Being "then" made free – then when? When they obeyed that form of teaching, and if you are in doubt regarding what that form of doctrine was, go back and reread Romans 6:3-5. They ceased being servants of sin and became servants of righteousness when they were baptized into Christ's death! They had changed masters (v.16).

Eph. 4:22-24

This is the second time that Paul uses this "old man – new man" analogy. He informs the Ephesians that the behavior (i.e., way of life; conduct) of Christians is to change from what it was prior to their conversion. They were to "put off" the old and put on the new. They were to be "*renewed in the spirit of their mind*" (v. 23). This reminds us of what he wrote to the Romans: "*be not conformed to this world: but be ye transformed by* **the renewal of your mind**..." (Rom. 12:2). We are to control our thought processes, for "*as a man thinketh in his heart, so is he*" (Prov. 23:7).

Putting on the new man requires "putting on" Christ (Gal. 3:27). They were to "put off" a number of bad behaviors, such as "lying, anger, theft (and replace it with honest work so we can help others), corrupt speech, bitterness, evil speaking, quarrelsome shouting, and all malice" (vss. 25-31).

Now that we are new persons, we are to be kind, tenderhearted, and forgiving (Eph. 4:32).

Col. 3:9

The third time the Apostle Paul uses the "old man – new man" contrast, he reminds the Colossians that they are *"risen with Christ"* and are to put to death such sins as fornication, covetousness, etc. i.e. things in which they once engaged before they became a new man (vss. 5-9). Why? Because they have *"put off the old man with his deeds,"* and have become the new man (v. 9). He then lists additional items which describe the new man they had become (vss. 12-17).

To sum up, let's remember that: "... *if any man be in Christ, he is a new creature: old things* (archaia here, probably due to the influence of the noun ktisis, which in the N.T. by metonymy is usually bears the notion of ktisma, creation - Robertson, Word Pictures, p. 239)) *are passed away; behold, all things are become new"* (2 Cor. 5:17). Now that we are new men and women, let's be careful that that we do not suffer a relapse (1 John 2:1-2), recalling that *"in due season we shall reap, if we faint not"* (Gal. 6:9).

Gems From The Greek

Made in the USA
Columbia, SC
24 February 2019